Solutions in Philosophy, Religious History, Literature, and Linguistics

CHARLES TUREK

University Press of America, Inc.
Lanham • New York • Oxford

Copyright © 2001 by
University Press of America,® Inc.
4720 Boston Way
Lanham, Maryland 20706

12 Hid's Copse Rd.
Cumnor Hill, Oxford OX2 9JJ

Library of Congress Cataloging-in-Publication Data

Turek, Charles
Solutions in philosophy, religious history, literature, and
linguistics / Charles Turek.
p.   cm
Includes bibliographical references (p.) and index.
1. Philology. 2. Philosophy. 3. Religion. I. Title.
P121 .T883   2000   001.3—dc21   00-048812 CIP

ISBN 0-7618-1884-7 (cloth: alk. paper)
ISBN 0-7618-1885-5 (pbk. : alk. paper)

Contents

Preface

I love philosophy, so seven of these eighteen essays have to do with this field. However, I got more pleasure out of writing on religious history, linguistics and literature. The reason for this is that these three disciplines deal with people more than philosophy does. In particular, when I wrote on literature I felt I was allowed to talk about myself.

I never planned these essays. The circumstances that led me to write some of them occurred accidentally. The essay on the Red Sea Crossing started after I had a chat in a religious bookstore with its employees and then bought a copy of the *Five Books of Moses*. The essay on sentences with symmetric verbs began when I attended a lecture by the linguist Ray Dougherty. After the lecture he gave me an article of his on this topic to read.

The essay on Donovan Joyce's book *The Jesus Scroll* was initiated when I spotted the book in a religious bookstore. I had never heard of the book up till then. Part of the essay on the syllogistic calculus came about after the philosopher, Fred Sommers, a former teacher of mine, unexpectedly sent me an article of his on this calculus, which, incidentally, he discovered.

The essay on the prayer scene in *Hamlet* originated in the following fashion: I had been reading the play over a period of days. During this time I myself was in a Hamlet-like situation, though I was not conscious of this. There were people in my life during this time who were like Claudius, Gertrude, Ophelia, Polonius and Horatio. I was like Hamlet!

Acknowledgments

Eight of these eighteen essays have been previously published. The author gratefully acknowledges the permission granted him by the following journals and magazines for allowing reprinting of previously published selections.

"Sommers, Waismann and Quine on Ambiguity," *The Incorporated Linguist* 4 (1972): 98-99

"A Note on Quine's Synonymy," *The Journal of Critical Analysis* 2 (1974): 85-86

"Lehmann on the Rules of the Invalid Syllogisms," *Notre Dame Journal of Formal Logic* 4 (1975): 603-604

"Basic Aristotelian Metaphysics," *The Philosopher* (The Philosophical Society of England) 12 (1978): 7-12

"Act V, Scene ii, Lines 410-415 in *Hamlet*" (entitled "Shakespeare's *Hamlet*" in the journal), *The Explicator* 2 (1986): 8-9

"The Red Sea Crossing and The Battle of Kadesh," *The Mediterranean* (a magazine) 1 (1987): 54

"The Origin of Symmetric Verb Sentences," *Grazer Linguistischer Studien.* University of Graz. Graz, Austria: (Autumn 1988): 115-124

"Is the Prayer Scene in *Hamlet* Part of the Plot?" (entitled "Shakespeare's *Hamlet*," in the journal), *The Explicator* 4 (1990): 239-241

Introduction

This book is a revised and expanded edition of my *Solutions in the Humanities, Revised and Expanded*, 1998.

These essays were written over the last twenty-eight years. Eight have been published before. Seven are on philosophy. They are : "Sommers, Waismann and Quine on Ambiguity," "A Note on Quine's Synonymy," "Lehmann on the Rules of the Invalid Syllogisms," "Basic Aristotelian Metaphysics," "Sommers' Syllogistic Calculus and Categories," "The Fields of Aristotelian Metaphysics," and "The Scientific Method in Linguistics and Literature."

An important task of logic is to determine whether an argument is valid or not. There are two grand calculi for doing this. One is the propositional-predicate calculus. The other is Fred Sommers' syllogistic calculus. My essay on Sommers' calculus was written partly around 1988 and partly in 1989. The last two-mentioned essays were written in 1996.

Two essays are on religious history. They are "The Historical Jesus According to Donovan Joyce's *The Jesus Scroll*," and "The Red Sea Crossing and the Battle of Kadesh." About nine years ago I saw a book in which the author cited Joyce's book and said it was fascinating. In 1973, a magazine, in its book review section, said Joyce's theory was preposterous. I side with the person who said the book was fascinating. It is my favorite book. My summary of it was written in 1986.

Five essays are on literature. They are: "Act V, Scene ii, Lines 410-415 in *Hamlet*," "Is the Prayer Scene in *Hamlet* Part of the Plot?," "What Was Hamlet's Reason for Putting on the Play?," "The Structure and Meaning of the To-be-or-not-to-be-Speech," and "When Did Hamlet Think of Putting on the Play?"

Introduction

Four essays are on linguistics. One is titled "The Origin of Symmetric Verb Sentences." The second essay on linguistics is "The Semantics of 'There Are' Sentences." It was written in 1995. The third essay is titled "More on 'There Are' Sentences." Part of it was written in 1997 and part of it was written in 1998. The fourth essay is titled "The Origin of Existential Sentences." It was written in May of 2000. Of the eighteen essays, this one is slowly becoming my favorite. After studying the topic of existential sentences for two or three years, I bought a book of literary criticism from a street vendor with the sole purpose of looking for existential sentences. To my surprise, the book had an unusual existential sentence. Once I studied this sentence, it took only a few minutes to arrive at the solution of the origin of existential sentences. The sentence was roughly "Nowhere is there a feeling of manipulation." As it is, I think this sentence was created by analogy.

The previous book had sixteen essays. This book has the same essays plus two more essays. I have added a sentence to the end of the essay on synonymy, and I have added a few words to the paragraph beginning with "In the Fourth Field" in *The Fields of Aristotelian Metaphysics*. I have added a sentence to the paragraph beginning with "Domains have auxiliary hypotheses" in *The Scientific Method in Linguistics and Literature*.

Chapter 1

ℰℭ

Sommers, Waismann and Quine on Ambiguity

F red Sommers[1] states, in effect, that if a, b, and c, are any three subjects and P and Q are predicates such that it makes sense to predicate P of a and b but not of c and it makes sense to predicate Q of b and c but not of a, then it must be that either P is ambiguous with respect to a and b, or Q is ambiguous with respect to b and c, or b is ambiguous with respect to P and Q.

One of Sommers' examples of this rule is:

(1)	(P) circular	(Q) memorized
apple	argument	phone number
(a)	(b)	(c)

Since "circular" makes sense of "apple" and "argument" but not of "phone number," and "memorized" makes sense of "phone number" and "argument" but not of "apple," either "circular," "memorized" or "argument" is ambiguous. However, if it assumed that the five words in this example are the only words in the English language, and if one asks oneself whether it is logically possible for each of the five words to have exactly one meaning, it will be seen that it would not be inconsistent to claim that (P), (Q) and (b) do not have to be ambiguous. (I adopt Sommers' rule in my essays on metaphysics in this book.)

One correct rule to detect ambiguity is that if a and b are any two subjects and P and Q are predicates such that it makes sense to predicate P of a and b and it makes sense to predicate Q of b but not a, and P and Q are synonymous, opposites or contraries with respect to b, then P must be ambiguous with respect to a and b.

Some examples are:

(2)		(P) big		(Q) large
	ballgame		house	
	(a)		(b)	
(3)		(P) big		(Q) small
	ballgame		house	
	(a)		(b)	
(4)		(P) big		(Q) medium-sized
	ballgame		house	
	(a)		(b)	

In all of these examples, (P) makes sense of (a) and (b), and (Q) makes sense of (b) but not of (a). If the four words in example (2), (3) or (4) were the only words in the English language, it would be possible for each of the words in these three examples to have one meaning. But once it is also given that (P) and (Q) in (2) are synonyms, then (P) is ambiguous; and once it is given that (P) and (Q) are opposites in (3), then (P) is ambiguous; and once it is given that (P) and (Q) are contraries in (4), then (P) is ambiguous.

W. Van Orman Quine[2] suggests that "hard" may be univocal with respect to "chair" and "question," and asks for evidence that "true" is ambiguous with respect to statements and confessions and that "exists" is ambiguous with respect to numbers and physical objects. Using the first correct rule for detecting ambiguity, it can be shown that at least "hard" is ambiguous. Since "hard" makes sense of "chair" and "question," and "difficult" or "easy" makes sense of "question" but not of "chair," then "hard" must be ambiguous with respect to "chair" and "question."

The above rule seems to be correct also in the cases when either P and Q are adverbs and a and b are adjectives, verbs, adverbs or sentences or when P and Q are prepositions and a and b are phrases or when P and Q are conjunctions and a and b are phrases and clauses.

In examples (2), (3) and (4) ambiguity is enforced in the predicate, but if one changes the rule from the predicates being synonyms, opposites or contraries to the subjects being synonyms, opposites, or contraries, you then detect ambiguity in the subject. Examples are:

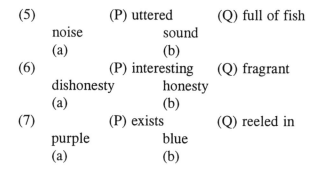

(5)   (P) uttered   (Q) full of fish
    noise   sound
    (a)   (b)

(6)   (P) interesting (Q) fragrant
    dishonesty   honesty
    (a)   (b)

(7)   (P) exists   (Q) reeled in
    purple   blue
    (a)   (b)

If in (5) it is given that (a) and (b) are synonyms, then it follows that (b) is ambiguous with respect to (P) and (Q). If in (6) it is given that (a) and (b) are opposites, then it follows that (b) is ambiguous with respect to (P) and (Q). (Honesty is a plant.) If in (7) it is given that (a) and (b) are contraries, then it follows that (b) is ambiguous with respect to (P) and (Q). ("Blue" is short for "bluefish.")

A third rule to enforce ambiguity is that if a makes sense of b and b makes sense of c but a does not make sense of c, then b is ambiguous with regard to a and c. For example, if "born ten years ago" makes sense of "prodigy" and "prodigy" makes sense of "flood" but "born ten years ago" does not make sense of "flood," then "prodigy" is ambiguous with respect to "born ten years ago" and "flood."

This rule can be extended. The extended rule is that if a and b make sense of c, and c makes sense of d and e, and a makes sense of d but not of e, and b makes sense of e but not of d, and if c is univocal with respect to a and d and with respect to b and e, then it follows that c is ambiguous not only with respect to a and e and with respect to b and d but also with respect to a and b and with respect to d and e. Here is an example:

(8) (a) born 10 years ago   (b) unforeseen
                (c) prodigy
    (d) John   (e) flood

If it is given that "born 10 years ago" makes sense of "prodigy" and "John" , but not of "flood," and "unforeseen" makes sense of "prodigy" and "flood" but not of "John," and "prodigy" makes sense of "John" and "flood," and if it is given that "prodigy" is univocal with respect to "born 10 years ago" and "John" and with respect to "unforeseen" and "flood," then "prodigy" is ambiguous not only with respect to "born 10 years ago" and "flood" and with respect to "unforeseen" and "John," but also with respect to "born 10 years ago" and "unforeseen" and with respect to "John" and "flood."

The idea for (8) originated with Friedrich Waismann.[3] In arguing for the ambiguity of the word "sign," he points out that people say the word "red" is a sign of color, and that swallows flying low is a sign of rain. He then says that when we say "red" is a sign of color, we are giving an explanation, and that when we say swallows are a sign of rain, we are stating a causal connection. Waismann goes on to say that an explanation is a convention, and that a convention can be broken or conformed to, but not proved or disproved, while a statement of a causal connection can be proved or disproved, but not broken or conformed to. Changing the wording around somewhat, it can be seen that his argument has the same form as (9):

(9)   (a) define   (b) predict
                    (c) sign
        (d) word   (e) event

Notice that in any example with the form of (8) or (9), if instead of being given that (c) is univocal with respect to (a) and (d), and to (b) and (e) it was given that (c) is univocal with respect to (a) and (b), and to (d) and (e), then in addition to (c) being ambiguous with respect to (a) and (e), and to (b) and (d), it would follow that (c) is ambiguous with respect to (a) and (d), and to (b) and (e). An example might be: (a) "harsh," (b) "defer," (c) "fine," (d) "person," (e) "show." Note that in this type of example (a) does not have to make sense of (d), and (b) does not have to make sense of (e). An example might be: (a) "green," (b) "torn," (c) "material," (d) "gain," (e) "values."

By extending Quine's request for evidence for detecting ambiguity in the terms "hard," "true" and "exist" to a request for evidence for detecting ambiguity in general, the above rules and examples may provide an answer to his request.

References

1. Sommers, Fred. "Predicability," *Philosophy in America*, ed. Max Black. Ithaca, New York: Cornell University Press, 1965, 262-281
2. Quine, Willard Van Orman. *Word and Object*, Cambridge, Massachusetts: MIT Press, 1960, 129-131
3. Waismann, Friedrich. *The Principles of Linguistic Philosophy*, ed. R. Harre. New York: St. Martin's Press, 127

Chapter 2

ฆ)ଔ

A Note on Quine's Synonymy

One of the things that Willard Van Orman Quine says in his *Two Dogmas of Empiricism* is the fact that two expressions can be interchanged without changing the truth-values of the statements in which they are interchanged does not mean that the two expressions are synonymous. One of his examples is "creature with a heart" and "creature with a kidney." These expressions are interchangeable because all creatures with a heart are creatures with a kidney and all creatures with a kidney are creatures with a heart. But notice that these co-extensive expressions and Quine's others - "Morning Star" - "Evening Star," "Scott" - "the author of Waverly," "nine" - "the number of planets" - (and even his "buffalo nickel" and "Indian nickel" in his *Word and Object*) are not words defined in the dictionary, nor should they, or must they, in some sense, be defined. It can be argued that the expression "Morning Star" is either like "ten story building" or "Mount Everest." Quine says that to consult a dictionary to determine synonymy is to beg the question, but after he says this he switches from words to non-words in evaluating the interchangeability criterion.

Even two expressions which he calls synonymous are not both words. He says that "bachelor" and "unmarried man" are synonymous.

"Bachelor" is a word. "Unmarried man" is not a word, and if it is short for a male adult not yet married, the meaning of "bachelor," then it is certainly not a word since we do not define meanings but words. The synonymy test can be looked upon as an attempt to show that "disavow" is a synonym of "repudiate" rather than to show that "deny responsibility for" is a synonym of "repudiate."

The expression "gold digger" can be regarded as a word when it means "a woman who associates with a man for material gain," but it does not have to be regarded as a word when it means "one who digs gold." The expression "thinking" might be ambiguous with respect to angels and persons since angels and persons are different types of things, but the expression "thinking about Vienna" is not ambiguous, or if it is ambiguous, it is ambiguous in a different way, or on a different level, from that of "thinking." In the same way the synonymy of meanings to the words they are meanings of, the synonymy of proper names to proper names, the synonymy of terms to terms, and synonymy of statements to statements are of a different kind, or on a different level, from that of the synonymy of words to words.

Now, I am wondering whether, after we refine the concept of a word, it will turn out that it is impossible, in principle, for there to be coextensive words (or at least whether they should be less in number than non-words). If we refine the concept of a word, and if it turns out that it is impossible for there to be expressions that are words to be coextensive, then the interchangeability criterion for synonymy on the level of words will be correct, and we will then be able to determine whether two words are synonymous without having to mention the meanings of any words. To put it another way, if meaning A and meaning B are two different meanings, then it is impossible for "all meaning A to be meaning B and all meaning B to be meaning A." Therefore, when at the level of words you *say* that all this (for instance, repudiating) is that (for instance, disavowing) and all that is this, you are required to admit that the two words are synonymous.

Sometimes a person says "All A is B but not all B is A" meaning that A and B have different meanings. This makes me think that the person would say they are synonymous if he thought all B is A.

Perhaps, there is another synonymy rule: If it follows that all A is D, when all A is B, and all C is D, then B and C are synonymous.

Chapter 3

ॐ

Lehmann on the Rules of the Invalid Syllogisms

A nne Lehmann[1] makes a distinction between valid, invalid, and neither valid nor invalid syllogisms. A valid syllogism is one in which the conclusion must be true when each of the two premises is true; an invalid syllogism is one in which the conclusions must be false when each of the two premises is true; a neither valid nor invalid syllogism is one in which the conclusion either can be true or can be false when each of the two premises is true. An example of a valid syllogism is: All M is P, All S is M, All S is P; an example of an invalid syllogism is: All M is P, Some S is M, No S is P; an example of a neither valid nor invalid syllogism is: All P is M, All S is M, Some S is not P.

As you may know, the "S" is called the minor term, the "P" the major term, and the "M" the middle term. The "S" term must always appear in the second premise and conclusion, and the "P" term in the first premise and conclusion. "Some M is P" and "All S is P" are called affirmative, and "Some S is not P" and "No S is P" negative. A term is either distributed or undistributed. If *all* is meant by a term, it is distributed, and if *some* is meant, it is undistributed; in All M is P, "M" is distributed and "P" undistributed; in No M is P, "M" and "P" are distributed; in Some S is P, "S" and "P" are undistributed; and in Some S is not P, "S" is undistributed and "P" is distributed (all P are not those some S). There are 256 syllogisms. With Lehmann, there are 24 valid syllogisms, 24 invalid, and 208 neither valid nor invalid. The valid and invalid syllogisms have the same set of premises, and their conclusions are contradictory to each other.

Those logicians who divide the 256 syllogisms into valid and invalid have come up with four rules, any one of which if violated by a syllogism means that the syllogism is invalid. Since Lehmann breaks up their invalid syllogisms into invalid and neither valid nor invalid, then if a syllogism violates one of the four rules it would not mean that it is invalid; it could be neither valid nor invalid. Therefore, she had to come up with rules of the invalid syllogisms. What I want to discuss is not the number of valid and invalid syllogisms she claims there are, but with the four rules of the invalid syllogisms that she comes up with.

First, I would like to say a word or two about the rules of the valid syllogisms which she quotes from a certain logic book. The four are: (1) Every valid syllogism has the middle term distributed at least once; (2) No term in the conclusion may be distributed unless also distributed in the premises; (3) No valid syllogism has two negative premises; (4) In a valid syllogism the conclusion may be negative if and only if one or the other premise is negative. The main thing that is wrong with these rules is that the first and third rules are descriptive and the second and fourth normative. Either all should be descriptive or all normative. The fourth rule should also be rephrased so as to reduce the risk of being counted as more than one rule. The rules rephrased descriptively are: (1) In each syllogism that is valid the middle term is distributed at least once; (2) In each syllogism that is valid the term when distributed in the conclusion is not undistributed in a premise; (3) In each syllogism that is valid there is at least one affirmative premise; (4) In each syllogism that is valid there is not exactly one negative statement.

Lehmann gives four rules of the invalid syllogisms. They are: (1) Every invalid syllogism has the middle term distributed at least once; (2) In an invalid syllogism no term is distributed in the conclusion and undistributed in the premises; (3) An invalid syllogism always has one and only one negative statement and exactly two affirmative statements; (4) One premise is negative only if the conclusion is affirmative; the conclusion is negative only when both premises are affirmative. One thing that is wrong with these rules is that the second rule is actually one of the four rules of the valid syllogisms. Another thing that is wrong is that the fourth rule can be deduced from the third rule. The rules should be: (1) In each syllogism that is invalid the middle term is distributed at least once; (2) In each syllogism that is invalid the minor term is distributed at least once; (3) In each syllogism that is invalid the major term is distributed at least once; (4) In each syllogism that is invalid there is exactly one negative statement.

Note that four is the minimum number and maximum number of rules in each of the two sets of rules. Note also that the logical structure is the same for each set—if a syllogism fits all four descriptions, then it is valid (invalid), and if it does not fit all four descriptions, then it is not valid (invalid).

We now have to draw up rules for the valid and invalid syllogisms as constructed by Fred Sommers.[2] He adds negative terms (for example, non-M), and then assigns the arithmetical plus and minus to all terms to compute validity.

References

1. Lehmann, Anne. "Two Sets of Perfect Syllogisms," *Notre Dame Journal of Formal Logic* 14 (1973): 425-429
2. Sommers, Fred. "The Calculus of Terms," *Mind* 79 (1970): 1-39

Chapter 4

౫౦ఁ౪

Basic Aristotelian Metaphysics

Metaphysics is the study of the different entities there are. For Aristotle, one of the main entities is species. Aristotle taught many things about species in three books—*Topics*, *Categories* and *Metaphysics*. One of the things that he taught (in *Topics*, Book 4, Section 3) is that there is more than one species for each genus there is. Since Aristotle taught about species, and to teach about species is to teach metaphysics, what Aristotle taught about species is called Aristotelian metaphysics. This paper mentions a few other things Aristotle taught in these three books, and also adds to what he taught.

The world contains things of different types and things of the same type. Stars, planets, rivers are different types of things. Siamese cats and Persian cats are the same type of thing. The world also contains parts of things. Parts of things are not things. Feet, surfaces, height are parts of things. Material (stuff out of which something is made) is neither a thing nor part of a thing. Water, leather, atoms are material.

There are two ways of describing things that are seen to be of different types and there are two ways of describing things seen to be of the same type. If two things are of different types, then the two things belong to two different nearest genera. If two things are of different types, and if two predicates are of two different types, then there will be at least one predicate that makes sense of the first thing but not of the second thing and there will be at least one predicate that makes sense of the second thing but not of the first thing. (I learned of this way of describing things of different types from the writings of Professor Fred Sommers.[1]) Trees and knives are different types of things. A tree is a plant and a knife is a cutting instrument. A plant and a cutting instrument are two different immediate genera. Since "shady" makes sense of trees but not of knives and "sharp" makes sense of knives, but not of trees, trees and knives are different types of things. If human beings and horses are different types, then "animal" cannot be their nearest genus and something must make sense of each one but not of the other. When two things are of the same type, then any predicate that makes sense of the first thing makes sense of the second thing and any predicate that makes sense of the second thing makes sense of the first thing. Collies and terriers are dogs. Whatever can be said of (makes sense of) a collie can be said of a terrier and whatever can be said of a terrier can be said of a collie. Collies and terriers are different kinds (of dogs) but are of the same type.

When two things are combined, we call the two things together a composite. A wader is a composite. It is a trouser and a boot. A trouser and boot are things of the same type. Trousers and boots are articles of clothing and an article of clothing is the nearest genus to trousers and boots. Therefore those philosophers who say that chairs and tables are of the same type are right because chairs and tables are articles of furniture. Whatever can be said of trousers can be said of boots and whatever can be said of boots can be said of trousers. A philosopher argued that trousers and boots are different types of things because you can say that a trouser has a 40-inch waist but you cannot say this of a boot whereas you can say a boot is high-heeled but you cannot say this of trousers. What is wrong here is that "has a 40-inch waist" and "high-heeled" are not legitimate predicates. A predicate cannot contain any reference to a part of a thing it is a predicate of because then it would be a predicate of the part, not of the thing. The heel is high, not the boot; the waist is 40 inches, not the trousers.

A suit is a composite—jacket and pants. A mule, a hybrid between a horse and a donkey, is a composite of two things of the same type.

Some philosophers say that a person is a composite of mind and body. Some say that a person possesses or has a body. I believe that neither view is correct. A person is (the generic "is") a body; he does not possess a body; and a mind is a part of a body. A body is not a thing or type of thing. It is a genus that is above types, or species. Nor are there individual minds and individual bodies at first separate but with some of the minds combining with some of the bodies later. Only types, or species, and kinds are things. Only types of things can form a composite. If someone says that a person possesses a body and also says that a body is part of a person, then we must ask him, "What is the other part?" because if a thing has a part, then it must have at least one other part, neither being a part of the other. But, as it is, even if he were forced to say that a person has another part, mind, and that this part was not a part of the part body, it would still not make a person a composite since parts are not things. Some philosophers not only say a person is a composite of mind and body but also say that minds and bodies are different types of things. But I believe that there are no things of different types in nature that combine.

A composite should not be defined as a thing that is composed of two or more types of things because it is incoherent to say this. When you define it this way, you are saying that a composite is three things—the thing, and two things. But the thing is not different from the two things; all you have are the two things. So a composite is not a thing, a single thing, but is a double thing. Therefore a composite should be defined as "two or more things, or species, combined."

It is impossible for a thing (a single thing, a non-composite) to have attributes of different types. For instance, if a tree can be said to be shady but a knife cannot be and a knife can be said to be sharp but a tree cannot be, then nothing can be shady and sharp. The formal rule (the rule was discovered by Sommers and is in his "*Predicability*;"[1] I am modifying it slightly) is: if there is a predicate P that makes sense of a word A that refers to a thing that exists or has existed but does not make sense of a word C that refers to a thing that exists or has existed and there is a predicate Q that makes sense of word C but not of word A, and predicates P and Q make sense of a third word B that refers to a thing that exists or has existed, then either the "thing" that word B refers to is a composite or predicate P is ambiguous or predicate Q is ambiguous or word B is ambiguous. For example:

	(P) shady	(Q) sharp	
(A) tree	(B) person		(C) knife

The word "shady" is ambiguous: "affording shelter from the sun's rays" and "of questionable merit;" and the word "sharp" is ambiguous, "having a thin keen edge" and "keen in intellect."

Note that since persons have to be of a different type from trees and knives, the example really has four predicates, but it is not necessary to actually mention four. Note, also, that just because trees and persons are different types of things does not mean that every predicate that makes sense of both is ambiguous—"white" is not ambiguous. Any predicate that makes sense of things of the same type is unambiguous, so mathematical statements and factual statements are true in the same sense (though statements are not things). The reason I said that the term (B) can refer to a composite is that man, I suppose, can combine two man-made physical objects of different types. The rule itself does not tell us that " shady" and "sharp" are ambiguous. Only observation tells us that. The rule only says that there must be ambiguity. It does not tell us which word is ambiguous, or which words are ambiguous. The rule has four predicates and three subjects. A second rule has three predicates and four subjects.

I said that it is impossible for a thing to have attributes of different types. I believe the following is proof: Aristotle in his *Metaphysics*, Book 5 defines contraries as attributes whose genera are different and as attributes which differ most within the same genus. So if two contraries, say, happy and sad, can make sense of the same thing, then two contraries that differ even more than these contraries cannot make sense of the same thing.

The ultimate genus is a "thing." A thing is an entity that itself is something or does something or is a whole. Men become philosophers and form corporations, armies, and countries, but there are not four additional species, or things; only man is a species and since you can only compare a thing with a thing, you cannot compare men with philosophers, armies, corporations and countries. A country is not a composite, even though a society is democratic but a territory is not while a territory is arable but a society is not and a country is democratic and arable. It is not a composite because a society is not a thing, or species. It also follows that it is not a thing and that a country is not a composite, because no two things of different types in nature combine. Events are not things; events befall things. So accidents, fires, lightnings, explosions, tides are not things.

Predicates must signify being something or doing something. The real predicate in "Those are interesting planets," "Those planets are interesting," and "Those planets interest people" is "is interested in" (planets), said of persons. It is not correct to say that each thing can be said to be interesting. The word "interesting" is not a predicate. The only predicate is "is interested in" and the only thing that this makes sense of is persons. The term "was discussed" is not a legitimate predicate. In "Planets were discussed" (by people) we are not saying what planets themselves are being or doing. A predicate must be in the active voice, not passive voice. The three entities we are comparing for compositehood or ambiguity must all be in the same category or mode—three materials, three parts, three things, three events. We cannot take two parts, say of a person, say that they are of different types, say that the differentiating predicates can be said of persons, point out that there is no ambiguity and that persons are not composites, and then claim the above first rule is incorrect.

There have been a few good counterexamples offered to the first rule. In other words, the attempt is to show that the same thing can have attributes of different types. One is that a headache can last an hour but a premise cannot while a premise can be confused but a headache cannot, yet a lecture can last an hour and be confused. What is wrong with this example is that two events, a headache and a lecture, are being compared with something, a premise, that is not an event. Also, "confused" may not be a proper predicate. Only persons are confused.

Another counterexample is: (A) "automobile," (P) "manufactured by General Motors," (B) "computer," (Q) "extracting a root," (C) "man." What is wrong here is that "manufactured by General Motors" is not a predicate since it is in the passive voice.

Another philosopher offered two counterexamples. One is that a motive is said to be altruistic but a pain is not while a pain is said to be intense but a motive is not, yet a desire is said to be both altruistic and intense. The other is that it makes sense to say of a squirrel that it ate a nut but it does not make sense to say this of mutual funds while it makes sense to say of mutual funds that it made a fortune in Xerox but it does not make sense to say this of a squirrel, yet it makes sense to say of a person that he ate a nut and made a fortune in Xerox. The answer to the first example is that a motive is a desire and this means that motives and desires are of the same type. (An entity and its nearest genus are of the same type.) A desire is a genus, not a type of thing. This is why it sounds strange to call a desire altruistic just as it would sound strange to say "That animal is a philosopher." What is wrong with the second example is that two physical objects, a squirrel and a person, are being compared with something, mutual funds, that is not a physical object. Also, "made a fortune in Xerox" is not a proper predicate for mutual funds since only people make money.

Another counterexample is: (A) "rock," (P) "heavy," (B) "man," (Q) "bankrupt," (C) "corporation." What is wrong with this example is that two physical objects, a rock and a man, are being compared with something, a corporation, that is not a physical object. Also, a corporation is not a thing. The final counterexample is: (A) "a headache," (P) "started at 3 p.m.," (B) "a parade," (Q) "was watched," (C) "a pretty girl." What is wrong with this example is that two events, a headache and a parade, are being compared with something, a pretty girl, that is not an event. Another thing wrong is that "was watched" is not a legitimate predicate.

Materials and parts are modes within the category thing. Events comprise another category. Since things cannot be compared with events (or acts) any predicate that makes sense of both must be ambiguous (a third rule). For example, "hard" makes sense of chairs and questions, and is ambiguous ("not easily penetrated" and "difficult to answer"). I believe that the word "exist" is not a proper predicate of anything outside the category of things since it is supposed to signify being or doing something.

Just as there is a hierarchy of genera, there is a hierarchy of predicates (see Sommers' *The Ordinary Language Tree*,[2] *Types and Ontology*,[3] and *Structural Ontology*[4]).

Each species is of a different type from at least one other species and is of the same type as at least one other species. Since there is a genus for each species, and there is more than one species for each genus, there is at least one species that each species is of the same type as. This means that man is or was the same type as at least one other species.

Since a predicate must signify being or doing, the denial of a predicate is not a legitimate metaphysical predicate. Therefore, non-green, not-exist, are not predicates, not attributes.

That it makes sense to say of a woman that she is pregnant but not of a man does not mean that one type of thing (persons) is two different types of things. The term "pregnant" is really being applied to a part of a person not to the person as a whole. It is like "high-heeled" in "The boot is high-heeled."

Since there is an ultimate genus, thing, there has to be an ultimate predicate. That predicate is "exist." It makes sense of every thing unambiguously.

The metaphysics we are discussing is not about individuals of a species since in order to know whether it makes sense to say of an individual that it is happy we first have to know of what species the individual is. Of course, if the individual is a person it will make sense to say of him that he is happy.

Aristotelian metaphysics is a system or science. One axiom is what a thing is. Another is what it is to be the same or a different type of thing. One theorem is that a thing cannot have attributes of different types. Another theorem is that things of different types in nature do not combine.

References

1. Sommers, Fred. "Predicability," *Philosophy in America*, ed. Max Black. Ithaca, New York: Cornell University Press, 1965, 262-281
2. _____. "The Ordinary Language Tree," *Mind* 68 (1959): 160-185
3. _____. "Types and Ontology," *Philosophical Review* 72 (1963): 327-363
4. _____. "Structural Ontology," *Philosophia* 1 (1971): 21-42

Chapter 5

ᏚᏬᏁᏅ

Act V, Scene II, Lines 410-415 in Hamlet

I have always believed that much of life is just knowing what somebody else is thinking. Shakespeare, in many scenes of his plays, likes to imply certain events took place before the scene in question opened. The question I would like to pose is: "Where in the text does it mean that Hamlet has just told Horatio that he thought it was Claudius he was stabbing behind the arras?" I look upon the question as an intellectual challenge, and the answer to it will reveal how another human being, Shakespeare, was being subtle.

In Act V, scene ii, 410-415, Horatio says:

> So shall you hear
> Of carnal, bloody, and unnatural acts,
> Of accidental judgments, casual slaughters,
> Of deaths put on by cunning and forced cause,
> And, in this upshot, purposes mistook
> Fall'n on the inventors' heads.

Now, what does "accidental judgments, casual slaughters" refer to? Well, what Horatio says can be divided into four "sentences," the first three beginning with the word "of" and the fourth "sentence" beginning with the word "and" and an implicit "of" before "purposes." Now, note that each of the "sentences" refers to one episode. The carnal, bloody, unnatural acts refer to Claudius' murder of Old Hamlet and seduction of Gertrude, all one episode. The deaths put on by cunning and forced cause refer to Hamlet's sending of Rosencrantz and Guildenstern to their deaths, all one episode. The purposes mistook fallen on the inventors' heads refer to Hamlet's not being aware of Claudius' and Laertes' real reason for having a duel and to the deaths of Claudius and Laertes, all one episode. Therefore, "of accidental judgments, casual slaughters" refers to Polonius' death and since the whole "sentence" refers to one episode, "accidental judgments" has to refer to Polonius' death too. So it refers to Hamlet's mistaking Polonius for Claudius.

The reason that the two nouns in "of accidental judgments, casual slaughters" are in the plural is that the nouns in the other "sentences" are in the plural. So please do not think that "slaughters" has to refer to more than one slaughter.

Notice that Horatio does not refer to the deaths of Ophelia and Gertrude, the two females, perhaps because they were not antagonists.

Now, after knowing what "accidental judgments, casual slaughters" refers to, take another look at what Horatio said, and you will notice that the first three "sentences" have something else in common besides each referring to one episode. Each of the first three "sentences" refers to what Hamlet has related to Horatio, and each of these three relatings is in the text of the play. Of course, Hamlet did not have to tell Horatio of the events referred to in the fourth sentence, since Horatio was a witness to them. The "carnal, bloody, and unnatural acts" was related in Hamlet's "One scene of it comes near the circumstance/Which I have told thee, of my father's death" in Act III, scene ii. The "deaths put on by cunning and forced cause" is Hamlet's telling of the Rosencrantz-Guildenstern incident to Horatio in Act V, scene ii. Now which words in the text constitute Hamlet's relating to Horatio the mistaking of Polonius for Claudius and the death of Polonius?

So much for this

These are the very first words of Act V, scene ii! The first two sentences are: "So much for this, sir; now shall you see the other/You do remember all the circumstance?" The "this" and the "other" are both circumstances. The circumstance that is the "other" is, of course,

Hamlet's sending of Rosencrantz and Guildenstern to their deaths, which Hamlet proceeds to relate. The circumstance that is the "this" is Hamlet's mistaking of Polonius for Claudius and killing of Polonius, which Hamlet is compelled to relate to Horatio so that Horatio would understand the reason for the recent scuffle he was involved in with Laertes.

Chapter 6

ℰↄℭℜ

The Historical Jesus According to Donovan Joyce's The Jesus Scroll

Finally, after almost two thousand years, someone has discovered the historical Jesus! That someone is Donovan Joyce. His book is *The Jesus Scroll*. The book came out in 1973. The publisher was Dial Press. It came out also in 1974. The publisher then was New American Library. The book was also brought out by Sphere Books (London) in 1975. No one, as far as I know, has ever mentioned Mr. Joyce or his book in any journal or book, and it is now 1986. The book, though, was reviewed in the October 1, 1973 issue of *Publisher's Weekly*, on page 70; in the October 6, 1973 issue of *America*, on page 250; and in the December 24, 1973 issue of *Time*, on page 55.

The world is coming closer and closer to what Mr. Joyce says, but I do not know if it will ever reach it. A problem has been solved, but people are still trying to solve it. It is for these reasons that I decided to write this paper. (I came across the 1974 book about fourteen years ago.)

In 1964, Mr. Joyce, an Irish Australian writer, went to Israel to write an historical novel mainly about Masada. In Tel-Aviv he met an archaeologist, who found a scroll at Masada. The archaeologist told Mr. Joyce that the scroll was written at Masada, that it described the imminent fall of the fortress, that it was written the night before that happened, that the author of the scroll identified the night as the eve of the Sabbath, that the author said he was eighty years old, and that he had a son who was crucified (at Masada, Joyce thinks). The archaeologist, a Max Grosset, who told Mr. Joyce that he had the Chair of Semitic Languages and Studies at some university in the United States, told Mr. Joyce that the author of the scroll said he had cut himself off from the world for many years and that he was the last descendant of the High Priest-Kings of Israel. Mr. Grosset told Mr. Joyce that these High Priest-Kings were the Hasmonean (or Maccabean) kings. Mr. Grosset told Mr. Joyce that the scroll was signed: Jesus of Gennesareth, son of Jacob. Mr. Grosset told Mr. Joyce that for two thousand years the world has known Jesus of Gennesareth as Jesus of Nazareth. Mr. Joyce does not know what happened to the scroll or to Mr. Grosset. From 1964 to 1972, almost eight years, Joyce did research. I will state his conclusions and his arguments for them. Note, his conclusions are based on his own research, not on what Mr. Grosset told him.

Joyce claims that Joseph probably divorced Mary (p. 39). Mary had been pregnant with Jesus but Joseph knew he was not the father. Matthew says that Joseph did not want to make Mary a public example, so he determined to put her away (divorce her) privily. Joyce accepts the truth of this, but denies Matthew's claim that Joseph later took Mary to himself, as though Joseph later forgave Mary. Joyce says that it was impossible for a Jew of those times to have done such a thing. The law of the Mishna compelled a man to divorce his wife for adultery publicly or privately or to denounce her publicly. Since Matthew says that at one point Joseph decided to divorce Mary privately, Joyce says we can only assume that this is what Joseph actually did.

Joyce suggests that Mary remarried (p. 40). The git, a secret bill of divorcement, allowed the guilty party to remarry. Joyce says that after Mary was divorced, she married Alpheus (p. 44). Mark and Matthew say that Mary the mother of James and Joses, the mother of Zebedee's children, and Mary Magdalene witnessed Jesus' crucifixion. John 19:25 says: "Now there stood by the cross of Jesus his mother, and his mother's sister, Mary the wife of Cleophas, and Mary Magdalene." Joyce says that the mother of Zebedee's children (Salome) and Mary's sister are the same person. Since John says Mary, Jesus' mother, was there, and John was an eyewitness, the Mary who is the mother of James and Joses is Jesus' mother, says Joyce.

Joyce assumes that there were exactly three women in this group of witnesses, which Mark and Matthew imply. This makes the Mary who is the wife of Cleophas one of the other three mentioned by John. Since she is not Mary Magdalene, and since she is not Jesus' mother's sister because sisters do not ususaly have the same first name, she and Jesus' mother are the same person. Joyce says that John 19:25 must have once read: "Now there stood by the cross of Jesus his mother Mary the wife of Cleophas, and his mother's sister, and Mary Magdalene." Therefore Mary married Cleophas. Cleophas and Alpheus are one and the same, says Joyce (p. 40). "Cleophas" (or "Clophas") derives from the Aramaic "Halphi," which is another form of the name "Alpheus," says Joyce (p. 40).

According to Joyce, Alpheus was Jesus' father. Paul in Galatians 1:18-19 said that he met James, the brother of Jesus. The Gospels also describe James as the son of Alpheus. Therefore Jesus was the son of Alpheus (p. 42).

According to Joyce, Alpheus was the brother of Joseph (p. 40). Joyce says Eusebius, the church historian, said that Hegesippus, the church historian, had said that Joseph had a brother whose name was Cleophas or Clophas.

Now the author of the scroll, Jesus of Gennesareth, signed his name as the son of Jacob, not as the son of Alpheus. Joyce, though, informs us that in the first century A.D. it was common practice for male Jews to adopt a Greek name for public use, and that they tried to take a Greek name that had the same meaning as their given Jewish name. The meaning of "Jacob" is "successor" and "successor" is also the meaning of "Alpheus," says Joyce (p. 45). This is one reason that makes Joyce think that Jesus is the author of that scroll. Another reason is that he sees that the name "Nazareth" is almost the same as the "nesareth" in "Gennesareth" (p. 180), and he believes that Nazareth did not exist in the time of Jesus (pp. 24-29).

Joyce believes that Jesus was an Hasmonean. The Hasmoneans traced their descent from Mattathias Hasmon, or Asmon, or Atsmon. The Hasmoneans regarded it as their duty to try to become Kings of Israel. Some of them were virtually King of Israel while at the same time they were High Priest. The last Hasmonean to attempt to become King of Israel was Simon ben Kosebar, who died in 135 A.D. The Hasmoneans were head of the course of Joarib, the first of the twenty-four courses of priestly families, and were the most important and powerful family in Israel. According to Joyce, Zacharias was an Hasmonean. Luke, in his first chapter, says that Zacharias, a priest, was of the course of Abia. Joyce denies this. He says that the course of Abia was excluded from the priesthood because it could not prove to the Jews who had returned to Jerusalem after the Babylonian captivity that it had been a priestly family (p. 61). Joyce says that the course of Abia had the same ancestor as the course of Joarib, and since Joarib was the course of the Hasmoneans, Zacharias was an Hasmonean (p. 61). Zacharias was the husband of Elizabeth, but Joyce says that the chances are that it was Zacharias, not Elizabeth, who was related to Jesus' parents. He states further that Zacharias was probably a cousin to Alpheus (and Joseph), not to Mary, since those things were only noticed through the male line. Therefore, it seems that Jesus was an Hasmonean. Zacharias' son, John the Baptist, was, therefore, also an Hasmonean.

Joyce would not be surprised if John the Baptist had wanted to become King of Israel. In the early first century the general meaning of "sacrament" was "soldier's oath of loyalty and allegiance." So Joyce suspects that John was forming an army (p. 69). When Jesus met John the two argued as to who should join whom — such is Joyce's reading of Matthew 3:13-15. Joyce says that the words that God is said to have used to show preference of Jesus to John derive from the second Psalm, which was the identical one used in the coronation ceremonies of the Hasmonean kings (p. 71). "Then Jesus was lead up by the Spirit into the Wilderness to be tempted by the devil" is construed by Joyce as Jesus' deliberating whether to do something that would assure his winning out over John for the Hasmonean throne.

Joyce argues that Jesus was married. In Jesus' time, says Joyce, every Jewish father was required to find a wife for his son. Not being married was a curse. A boy was expected to be married between the ages of sixteen and twenty (p. 77). Luke 8:1-3 says ". . . many women who ministered unto him of their substance." Joyce says that if Jesus were unmarried then what he was doing was not sanctioned by the Law in first century Judaism (p. 78). John 2:1-2 says ". . . there was a marriage in Kana of Galilee, and the mother of Jesus was there; and both Jesus was called, and his disciples to the marriage." Joyce points out that John said that Jesus was "called," not invited. A person who was going to get married and was travelling in the countryside was called or summoned to his wedding so that he would not forget about it (p. 81).

Joyce estimates the wine at the wedding at 1,080 pints, which is equivalent to 90 dozen bottles of claret, enough for about 1,000 people. Joyce suggests that this was Jesus' wedding and that it was held at Kana because it was obligatory for the heir to the Hasmonean throne to be married in the presence of the chief men of the Joarib clan; and Kana was the feudal base of the Hasmoneans. When Jesus returned home late to Bethany to see Lazarus, Martha was furious and ran out of the house and upbraided Jesus. When Martha went back into the house she said to Mary of Bethany, her sister: "The Master has come and calls you." Then Mary arose quickly and went to Jesus. Joyce says that in those days a husband who was returning home sent for his wife, and until he did so, his wife sat in the house. This is what Mary did, and when she went to Jesus she called him "Baal," which can mean either "Lord" or "husband." On another occasion, Jesus arrived at the house in Bethany and Mary promptly sat at his feet (Luke 10:38-42). Joyce points out that married men are familiar with this intimacy. While they sat like that, Martha, who was preparing a meal all by herself, complained to Jesus that Mary was not helping her. Joyce says that since Martha complained to Jesus rather than Mary, it was Jesus, not Martha, who had control and authority over Mary (p. 87).

On Saturday night, the eve of Palm Sunday, Mary of Bethany annointed Jesus with spikenard. Joyce informs us that the manufacture and possession of spikenard was severely restricted. Its use was strictly reserved by the law to the anointing of the Kings of Israel. Therefore, Mary of Bethany would not have dared to have it in her hand unless she was the wife of a royal personage (p. 92). Now Joyce also argues that Mary Magdalene may have been Jesus' wife. Some time after she finds the tomb empty, she sees Jesus and addresses him as Lord or husband (p. 87). The *Gospel of Mary*, discovered in Egypt in 1896, suggests that if they were not man and wife, they should have been. One part of the fragments of the *Gospel of Philip*, discovered around 1946, says "There were those who walked with the Lord at all times, Mary his mother, and her sister (Salome) and Magdalene, this one who is called his partner." In the very next sentence, the Magdalene is referred to as Jesus' "spouse." Joyce says on page 87 that it must remain inconclusive that Mary of Bethany and Mary Magdalene were the same person. On page 92 he says ". . . Mary of Bethany, who, we say, was his wife and Mary called Magdalene under another name."

Joyce argues that Jesus had a son. In the days of Jesus, childlessness was a mark of God's distinct disfavor (p. 77). Joyce suggests that it was

Barabbas who was Jesus' son. Jerome, the great scholar and Father of the early Church, writing in the fourth century A.D., uses the phrase - taken from the long lost *Gospel of the Hebrews* - "filius magistri eorum," which translates from Latin into "the son of their teacher or master;" and that Jerome says in the gospel the given name of this man Bar Abbas was Jesus (p. 97). Since Barabbas' first name was Jesus, Joyce thinks that Jesus had a son and gave his son the same name that he had. Joyce also suggests that the name "Barabbas" was formed from "bar Abbas" which means "son of the master," and that this also makes Joyce suspect that Barabbas was the son of Jesus. Of course, Joyce thinks that the son of the Jesus of Gennesareth of the scroll is Barabbas (p. 99).

Joyce says that the anointing of Jesus by Mary of Bethany was a symbolic politico-religious ceremony, which makes it quite certain that when Jesus was cleansing the Temple, he was making a bid to capture Jerusalem and to restore the Hasmonean throne (pp. 92-93). Joyce says that Jesus led an armed force. He says that tradition puts the number of armed supporters at 4,000. A lost work by Josephus, of which we have a medieval Hebrew copy, puts their total at 2,000. Sossianus Hierocles, the Roman procurator of Phoenicia, Arabia Libanitis and Bithynia, says that Jesus led a band of "highway robbers" numbering more than 900 men (p. 93). The reason that Jesus chose to attack on Sunday was that there would be less troops to fight. Pontius Pilate, with a cohort (500 men), and Herod Antipas, with a cohort, were not going to arrive before the middle of the week. There were only the Jewish Temple Police numbering no more than 200 men and one cohort of Roman troops in Jerusalem on Sunday. Jesus, though, was defeated. He retreated to Bethany. Barabbas, his son, was captured. Joyce's quote (p. 95) of Mark 15:7 is: "And there was one named Barabbas, which lay bound with them that had made insurrection with him, who had committed murder in the insurrection." Note Joyce's "with him."

Joyce says that Jesus hung around Bethany rather than simply escaping because his son Barabbas had been captured. Joyce says that Judas was arrested and later was let go to tell Jesus *that his son would be allowed to go free if he would give himself up* (p. 98). Joyce says that Jesus decided to announce his decision to his disciples and to the Hasmoneans at what is called the Last Supper (p. 101).

Joyce says that since Jesus went to the cross on Friday he could not have eaten the Passover on Thursday. This was an impossible act for an orthodox Jew because the orthodox passover began Friday night that year.

Joyce says that Jesus celebrated the Passover of the Essenes. The Essene Sabbath fell on Wednesday, not on Saturday, and the Essene Passover always fell on the Wednesday Sabbath. Therefore, Jesus ate the Passover on Wednesday night.

Jesus decided to give himself up and to be arrested at the Garden of Gethsemane. Judas was sent to convey the decision. This is how it came about that Jesus knew beforehand when and where he would be arrested. This is why Jesus was waiting in the Garden of Gethsemane to be arrested rather than simply escaping. Judas never betrayed him. Judas was only a messenger.

Jesus devised a plan to survive the crucifixion. The main idea was to work it out so that he would be on the cross the least amount of time. What Jesus did was to draw out the trials with the result that he was crucified three hours before the Sabbath (p. 20). By being crucified only three hours before the Sabbath, the Romans were forced to bind Jesus' wrists rather than nail them. Nailing was for victims they wanted to suffer for up to six days (p. 17; Joyce says nearly seven days on p. 107). With binding, the victim only suffered a few hours, but since the victim was still alive after a few hours, his legs were clubbed. In about an hour, the victim died (p. 19). Part of Jesus' plan was to be drugged so that he would look dead to the executioner. The sponge offered Jesus when he was on the cross was soaked in vinegar and gall. The vinegar was sour red wine, the gall was opium (p. 108). Joyce says that John, who was an eyewitness, may have mistaken the vinegar on Jesus' body for blood and therefore thought that the spear which was just used to hold the sponge for Jesus had at some point been thrust into Jesus' side. Since there was only one hour left before the Sabbath, and since the Romans obeyed the Jewish law that no one stay on the cross on the Sabbath, the executioner clubbed the legs of the two crucified with Jesus, but when he came to Jesus he thought Jesus was dead, and so he did not club Jesus' legs (p. 20). Jesus' plan called for Joseph of Arimathea to take down his body at this point, so Joseph went to Pilate to ask for the body of Jesus. Joyce says that Joseph and Pilate talked in Greek, and that Joseph said "soma," which means "body" in Greek. Pilate corrected him by saying "ptoma," which means "corpse" in Greek. However, the centurion, who thought that Jesus was dead, told Pilate that Jesus was dead. So Joseph was permitted to take down the body of Jesus.

Joyce argues that Jesus was not dead from the fact that it was Joseph, not the executioner, who took down the body. The Law of Judaism commanded that no Jewish male should come at a dead body except if the male was the victim's closest available eldest relative. Joyce says that because of this, it can be confidently asserted that Jesus was not dead (p. 128).

Jesus was crucified at Golgotha. John 19:41 (Joyce had 19:40 on p. 119) describes it: "Now in the place where he was crucified there was a garden, and in the garden a new sepulchre wherein was never man yet laid." Joyce says that since there was a garden this was not a site for public executions. So Jesus was crucified in a private place, which was also part of Jesus' plan (p. 119). The Gospels say "Golgotha" means in Hebrew "The Place of a Skull," but "Golgotha" does not mean that, says Joyce. He says (pp. 121-123) that "skull" in Hebrew is "gulgoleth" and that "Golgotha" means "wheel-like stone disc for squashing aromatic oil of plants" ("gol") and "a press" ("geth"). Joyce argues that Golgotha was in the Garden of Gethsemane. He says reference books say "Gethsemane" means "press olive oil." Joyce says "semane" does not mean "olive oil;" "shemen sayith" does. Joyce says "samane" means "jasmine." He also points out that "Gethsemane" is called "el Jesmaniyeh" in Arabic. Joyce concluded that the Garden of Gethsemane was once known as the Jasmine Garden, and further, that the colloquial name for the Jasmine Garden was "Golgeth," since the jasmine was treated with a wheel press.

Joyce believes that Joseph of Arimathea was an Hasmonean, and that he almost certainly owned the Garden of Gethsemane (p. 129). Joyce, on page 53, says the Garden of Gethsemane was in The King's Garden and that The King's Garden was owned by the Hasmoneans.

After Joseph of Arimathea took Jesus down from the cross, he took Jesus to the tomb, which Joyce says was in the Garden of Gethsemane. Jesus was revived. He later came upon Mary Magdalene (p. 139). Joyce believes that Jesus went to live with the Essenes at Qumran (p. 139). He thinks Jesus fled to Masada in 68 A.D., when the Romans attacked Qumran. Joyce believes that one of the thousand that died at Masada in April of 73 was Jesus.

Chapter 7

ℰℭℛ

The Red Sea Crossing and the Battle of Kadesh

I f you take a look at the account of the Battle of Kadesh and the account of the Red Sea Crossing you will see that the story of the Red Sea Crossing (in the *Book of Exodus* in The Old Testament) was taken from the story of the Battle of Kadesh!

The Battle of Kadesh was between the Egyptians and the Hittites around 1285 B.C. Kadesh was a few miles north of Damascus. The Egyptian king was Ramses II. The Hittite king was Muwatalish (or Metella).

The Battle of Kadesh was depicted on the walls of at least five Egyptian temples. A modern translation of the inscriptions is in *Ancient Egyptian Literature* (Vol. II, 1976), by Miriam Lichtheim. A commentary by James Henry Breasted appears in the *Decennial Publications of Chicago University* (Series 1, vol. V, 1927). Breasted also wrote about the battle in his book, *History of Egypt* (1909).

I will only point out the most important similarities. Breasted says on page 43 of his commentary ". . . the river is swelled and widened, perhaps by a dam, which backs up the water from below, with the intent of strengthening the city's defenses. The line of the water at the bottom may be the brook of El-Mukadiyeh." And in a footnote on the same page "this backed-up water . . . is filled with escaping men and horses . . ." Breasted is describing a scene that is drawn on a wall of the temple of Ramesseum. According to *Baedeker's Egypt 1929* (p. 326), it seems to be in the Second Court, front wall, Lower Row. The river is the Orontes River. The line drawing of this scene is on page 452 of Breasted's book and is Plate III of his commentary. It is also on two glass-covered tables in the Egyptian exhibit in the Metropolitan Museum of Art in Manhattan - one table at the entrance to the exhibit and one at the 19th dynasty exhibit. It is also in the *Atlas of Ancient Egypt* (pp. 202-203), which is in the museum's bookshop. The scene shows Ramses II single-handedly defeating the Hittite chariotry. Ramses II is in his chariot. He is aiming his bow and arrow at the Hittites. The Hittites are falling into the Orontes River. Some are being pulled out by their fellow soldiers. One after being pulled out (the chief of Aleppo) is turned upside down so that he may disgorge the water he swallowed. What caught my eye in the commentary was the "backed-up water" and the "perhaps by a dam." In the *Book of Exodus* it says:

> And Moses stretched out his hand over the sea;
> and the Lord drove back the sea with a
> strong east wind all that night, and made the sea
> dry land, and the waters were split (Ch. IV, 21).

Notice "back" and "split." Now verse 22:

> And the children of Israel went into the midst of
> the sea on dry ground; and the waters were a wall to them, on their right
> and on their left.

Notice the word "wall." Of course, the Hittites' being in danger of drowning in the Orontes River is parallel to the Egyptians' drowning in the Red Sea.

The temple inscriptions say that Ramses II single-handedly defeated the Hittites. The *Book of Exodus* portrays Moses single-handedly defeating the Egyptians.

The Battle of Kadesh contains a poem. The Red Sea Crossing contains a song.

By knowing about the Battle of Kadesh it is easier to understand the story of the Red Sea Crossing. For instance, does the *Book of Exodus* say that the whole Egyptian army drowned? Ch. IV, 28 says:

> And the waters returned, and covered the
> chariots, and the horsemen with all the host of
> Pharaoh that came after them into the sea; there
> remained of them not even one.

This sounds as though it were saying the whole Egyptian army drowned, but verse 23 says:

> And the Egyptians pursued, and went in after
> them, all Pharaoh's horses, his chariots, and
> his horsemen, to the midst of the sea.

And verse 24 says:

> And it came to pass in the morning watch, that
> the Lord looked at the camp of the Egyptians
> with the pillar of fire and of the cloud and
> brought to confusion the camp of the Egyptians.

And verse 25 says:

> And he took off the wheels of their chariots, and
> caused them to move onward with
> difficulty; and the Egyptians said, Let us flee
> from the face of Israel; for the Lord fights
> for them against the Egyptians.

Now how can the pursuing Egyptians of verse 23 be the ones in the morning watch of verse 24? The author of the *Book of Exodus* is distinguishing two groups of Egyptians - those that were with the Pharaoh and those that made up the camp. The camp of the Egyptians fled from the Israelites. So the Egyptians that made up the camp did not drown. All this is known by knowing about the Battle of Kadesh.

Ramses II started out from Egypt with four divisions. The four divisions were Amon, Re, Ptah and Sutekh. The four divisions marched in that order. Ramses II led the first division — the division of Amon.

When he reached Shabtuna, a few miles south of Kadesh, the Hittites sent some spies to him and made him think that they were at Aleppo, a few miles north of Kadesh. Ramses II then led the first division to the west of Kadesh, and they camped there. The division of Re was still further south and the divisions of Ptah and Sutekh even further. Later, outside Kadesh, Hittite spies were captured and they confessed that the Hittite army was on the east side of Kadesh. At this point, the Hittite chariotry attacked the division of Re. Then the Hittite chariotry attacked the division of Amon. This is the point where, according to Ramses II, the division of Amon deserted him, and he single-handedly defeated the Hittites and drove many of them into the Orontes River. It is this distinguishing between Ramses II and his camping division of Amon and the division's desertion of Ramses II that enable us to realize that the author of the *Book of Exodus* is distinguishing between those that were with the Pharaoh and the camp of the Egyptians and that the "Let us flee from the face of Israel" of verse 25 is saying that the camp of the Egyptians deserted the Pharaoh.

Perhaps the account of the Red Sea Crossing can help Egyptologists learn more about the Battle of Kadesh.

This leaves open the question of when and how the Israelites escaped from Egypt. At present, scholars believe the Israelites escaped during the reign of Ramses II (1290-1224 B.C.).

Chapter 8

෪‍ଔ

The Origin of Symmetric Verb Sentences

In this paper on syntax I show that the sentences in the domain of symmetric verb sentences were created by analogy, deletion, blending, borrowing and replacing.

1. The Derivation

In the beginning, there were sentences like

(1) John is good
(2) John loves Mary
(3) John is similar to Mary
(4) John kissed Mary

Now the verb *to kiss* is not symmetric. However, there had to be symmetric kissing in the beginning. The sentence to report a symmetric kiss seems to have been sentence (5)

(5) John kissed Mary and Mary kissed John

A certain period of time passed after these five sentence forms and others were created and then sentences of the form

(6) John and Mary kissed each other

were created. Sentence (6) is synonymous with sentence (5).

After sentence form (6) was created a certain period of time passed and there was created sentence form (7)

(7) John and Mary are similar to each other

This sentence form was created from sentence form (6) by analogy. We imitated the form of (6) to create the new form (7). The form of (6) is a subject composed of two singular noun phrases joined by *and*, a semi-symmetric verb meant symmetrically, and *each other*. The form of (7) is the same except for the verb, which is symmetric. We broke or extended the rule that had allowed a sentence such as (6). We knew that verbs like *to be similar* (I call them verbs for the sake of an easy flow of discussion) do not have the same property that verbs like *to kiss* have. Verbs like *to be similar* are symmetric while verbs like *to kiss* are semi-symmetric. In (3) and (7), Mary must be similar to John every moment he is similar to her, whereas in (4) Mary had to kiss John only at least one moment out of all the moments he kissed her.

A certain period of time passed after sentence form (7) was created and then there was created sentence form (8)

(8) John and Mary are similar.

As Gleitman[1] says, sentences like (8) were created by deleting the preposition and *each other* in sentences like (7). Note that if the verb is not symmetric you cannot delete anything. For example, *live with* in (9)

(9) John and Mary live with each other

is a symmetric predicate but since *live* is not symmetric we cannot delete anything.

A certain amount of time passed after sentences such as (8) were created. Then sentences with the form

(10) John and Mary kissed

were created. Sentence forms like (10) were created from sentence forms like (8) by analogy. Note that, though, (8) came from (7), (10) did not come from (6). Sentence (10), though synonymous with (6), did not come from (6) since *each other* was needed in (6) to make the verb *kissed* symmetric. If you had taken away the *each other* you would have been left with a verb that is not symmetric. After sentences such as (8) were created, there was something to make the verb symmetric.

2. The Evidence for the Theory

Now I would like to offer evidence for my theory. There are no counterexamples. All exceptions are explained (below). But the main evidence for the hypotheses of the theory is that there is something wrong with all other hypotheses.

Now let us look at the theory of Lakoff and Peters.[2] They argue that a sentence such as (11)

(11) John is similar to Mary

came from a sentence such as (12)

(12) John and Mary are similar

They state, correctly, that a sentence such as (13)

(13) John left with Mary

is symmetric, but they believe that *Mary* in (13) is part of the real subject and that therefore (13) came from (14)

(14) John and Mary left

They then reason that since (13) is symmetric, all symmetric sentences with the form of (11) came from sentences with the form of (12). As to how we got from (12) to (11), they said we added *to* before *Mary*, then moved *to Mary* to the right of *similar*, and then deleted *and*. One thing wrong with this analysis is that (14) is not symmetric even with the meaning that John and Mary left together (see below on *to be together*), and therefore

(13) did not come from (14). A second thing wrong is that if (13) came from (14), then (15)

(15) John lived with Mary

would have had to come from (16)

(16) John and Mary lived

But (15) could not have come from (16) since it is not synonymous with (16). A third thing wrong is that a sentence form such as (17)

(17) John agreed with Bill

could not have come from a sentence such as (18)

(18) John and Bill agreed

since (17) is semi-symmetric, while (18) is symmetric.
    Lakoff and Peters argued that (19)

(19) John and Bill are similar

did not come from (20)

(20) John and Bill are similar to each other

They thought that (21)

(21) John and Bill killed Harry

is symmetric, and since (21) does not come from (22)

(22) *John and Bill killed Harry with each other

because (22) is ungrammatical, they concluded that (19) did not come from (20). They were not aware of the fact that (21) is not symmetric even when it means that John and Bill together killed Harry.

Lakoff and Peters gave an explanation for the origin of (23)

(23) John and Bill are similar to each other

They suggested that possibly there was first (24)

(24) John and Bill are similar and Bill and John are similar

Then from this they suggest came (25)

(25) John is similar to Bill and Bill is similar to John

and from this they suggest came (23). (Gleitman also says that (23) came from (25).) Obviously, (24) and (25) could not be the cause of (23) since they have never been events, since they have never existed.

I cannot give any literary evidence for this theory. The earliest body of Old English literature dates from the 700's A.D.

3. More of the Theory

I do not know if sentence (6) came from sentence (5) or if there were intervening sentences.

Sentences (3), (7) and (8) are synonymous. Sentence (4) is not synonymous with either (5), (6) or (10). Sentences (5), (6) and (10) are synonymous.

Sentences (5) and (6) are ambiguous. They have a meaning that is symmetric and a meaning that is not symmetric.

Other verbs like *to kiss* are *to argue, to agree, to fight, to embrace,* and, perhaps, *to collide* and *to meet.* Semisymmetric verbs refer to actions that a person can start or end before another does.

It seems that verbs such as *to mix, to combine, to join* are sometimes symmetric and sometimes semisymmetric.

It just may be that all symmetric and semisymmetric verbs were once followed by a preposition. Most still are.

We imitated sentences like (6) to create sentences like (7). The reason we created sentences like (7) may have been that since the verb in sentences like (3) is symmetric we felt that neither individual referred to in such sentences is entitled to be the subject more than the other.

Other verbs like *to be similar* are *to be synonymous, to be the contradictory, to be the contrary, to be different, to be the same, to be equivalent, to bear a resemblance, to distinguish.*

The following verbs are not symmetric: *to spread out, to disperse, to assemble, to be heterogeneous, to be birds of a feather, to be a pair, to be two of a kind, to be one and the same, to be twins, to be brothers, to be shipmates.* The first four are collective verbs and so cannot take singular, concrete nouns for subjects. Collective verbs are not symmetric because they are predicated within the subject, not outside the subject, and so the subjects are not being related to something else. The last seven are additive verbs but are also not symmetric because the singular, concrete nouns of their subjects are not being related to each other. For example, in sentence (26)

(26) John and Bill are twins

the verb *to be twins* is not symmetric since it asserts that John came from a certain birth and that Bill came from that birth, and to do this is not to relate John and Bill to each other. Note that we also say that

(27) John is a twin

meaning by this that John is one of two. This shows that we are also asserting in (26) that John and Bill are two, and to say that John and Bill are two is not to relate John and Bill. The dictionary defines "twin" as "either of two offspring produced at a birth." Hence "to be a twin" is not a relation, and since symmetric verbs express relation, "to be a twin" is not a symmetric verb.

Dougherty[3] thought that

(28) John and Bill are birds of a feather

is a counterexample to Gleitman's theory. He thought that *to be birds of a feather* is symmetric and that since (28) does not come from (29)

(29) *John and Bill are birds of a feather with each other

since (29) is ungrammatical, he thought that Gleitman's theory that sentences such as (8) come from sentences such as (7) is not correct.

However, her theory is correct for the simple reason that *to be birds of a feather* is not symmetric. The verb is like the verb *to be two of a kind*. The verb *to be two of a kind* asserts that a thing is of a certain kind and that a second thing is of that kind, and to assert this is not to relate the two things.

Some time after writing this paper I came across a sentence with the verb "to be birds of a feather." The sentence is "Arthur in King John is a bird of another feather..." This shows that the verb is not symmetric. (The sentence is on page 28 of Edward Wagenknechts' *The Personality of Shakespeare*, University of Oklahoma Press, 1972.)

Massey[4] thought that *to be shipmates* is symmetric. However, for the same reason that *to be twins*, *to be birds of a feather*, and *to be two of a kind* are not symmetric, *to be shipmates* is not symmetric.

Sentence (30)

(30) John, Bill, and Mary are similar

seems to be a blend of

(31) John and Bill are similar

and

(32) John, Bill and Mary are linguists

A sentence such as (33)

(33) John is like a lion

is not symmetric since it does not relate an individual person to an individual lion.

A sentence such as (34)

(34) John and Mary live together

is not symmetric. The meaning of *together* is *in one place*, and this meaning is not symmetric. Therefore this sentence is not a counterexample to Gleitman's theory. Note that sentences (9) and (34) are not synonymous! It may be that a sentence such as (34) has a symmetric meaning now. But it does not matter what meaning it has now. What matters is what meaning it had in the beginning since syntax is the study of the origin of sentences; and the meaning it had in the beginning was not symmetric.

4. The Exceptions

There are some exceptions to Gleitman's theory. Some are: *to be like*, *to be opposite*, *to be near*, *to be far*, *to be beside*. The reason that (35)

(35) *John and Mary are beside

is ungrammatical while (36)

(36) John and Mary are beside each other

is grammatical is that *beside* is a preposition in (35) — and so would *like, opposite, near, far* be — and prepositions cannot occur without an object.

Other exceptions are: *to contradict* (said of sentences), *to equal*, *to encounter* (if one of its meanings is symmetric), *to resemble*.

Sentence (37)

(37) John and Mary resemble each other

is grammatical but sentence (38)

(38) *John and Mary resemble

is ungrammatical. I believe I can explain why (38) is ungrammatical. It happens that the English borrowed the word *resemble* in the 12th century from the French who had settled in England after the Norman Conquest. The French verb is *se ressembler*. The reflexive pronoun *se* means *each other*. In French, there is a rule that if a symmetric verb takes *se*, *se* cannot be deleted. We must have borrowed this rule. I would also say that all other symmetric verbs that are exceptions to Gleitman's theory were borrowed from French.

Sentence (39)

(39) John and Mary are alike

came from (40)

(40) *John and Mary are alike to each other

before (40) became ungrammatical. Sentence (40) became ungrammatical because after *resemble* was borrowed, it replaced *to be alike*. Since (38) was ungrammatical, (39) continued.

5. Conclusion

Elliott[5] informs us that an inscription on the Franks casket, in the runic alphabet and Old English of the early 8th century, reads literally

(41) Here fight Titus and Jews

This means that sentence form (10) was created at least 1,200 years ago.

References

1. Gleitman, Lila. "Coordinating Conjunctions in English," *Language* 41 (1965): 282
2. Lakoff, George and Stanley Peters. "Phrasal Conjunction and Symmetric Predicates," *Modern Studies in English*, ed. David A. Reibel and Sanford A. Schane. Englewood Cliffs, New Jersey: Prentice-Hall, 1969, 113-142
3. Dougherty, Ray C. "A Survey of Linguistic Methods and Arguments," *Foundations of Language* 10 (1973): 430f.
4. Massey, Gerald. "Tom, Dick, and Harry and all the King's Men," *American Philosophical Quarterly* 13 (1975): 89-107
5. Elliott, Ralph Warren Victor. *Runes*. New York: Philosophical Library, 1959, 101

Chapter 9

ഇ)൧

Is the Prayer Scene in Hamlet *Part of the Plot?*

As it stands now, *Hamlet* does not make sense. (I will be quoting from the Folger Library Edition.) There are two inconsistencies in the scene in which Hamlet supposedly runs into Claudius praying. One is that the text has Hamlet running into Claudius and then going on to have a talk with Gertrude, his mother. Claudius has arranged for Polonius to eavesdrop behind the arras. When Hamlet hears a stirring, he stabs the figure, thinking it is Claudius ("I took thee for thy better," Act III, scene iii, 39). But how could Hamlet have thought that he had killed Claudius if he had just left him praying? Hamlet had left the scene before Claudius and so would have arrived at his mother's closet before him. Hamlet would not expect Claudius to have gotten there first.

The other inconsistency is that the text has Hamlet in a mood to kill Claudius ("Now could I drink hot blood," Act III, scene ii, 397). But soon after, Hamlet runs into Claudius praying and then supposedly gives himself excuses for not killing him. The question is, then how could Hamlet be in a mood to kill Claudius one minute and not be in a mood to kill him the next?

The text has Hamlet say:

I'll have these players
Play something like the murder of my father
Before mine uncle. I'll observe his looks,
I'll tent him to the quick; if he but blench,
I know my course.

(Act II, scene ii, 602-606)

These lines constitute the reason that Hamlet is putting on the play *The Murder of Gonzago*. However, as he has already asked the player (at Act II, scene ii, 543-44) to put on the play, he really had the reason for putting on the play at that point, and not at 602-606. The reason for putting on the play was not stated at lines 543-544. Instead, it comes two pages later, via a literary device that was current in Shakespeare's time, and that was not to be counted one of the events of the plot:

I have heard
That guilty creatures, sitting at a play,
have by the very cunning of the scene
Been struck so to the soul that presently
They have proclaimed their malefactions;
For murder, though it have no tongue, will speak
With most miraculous organ.

(596-602)

Note the inconsistency between the lines that constitute the reason and "About, my brain!" (line 596). The latter says that Hamlet is thinking lines 596-606 now. But because we know that Hamlet had the reason before, the event referred to by the literary device is not really happening. It is not to be counted one of the events of the plot.

Let us take a look at the structure of this part of Act II, scene ii. There are certain lines within a soliloquy that by themselves have a meaning from which it can be determined that they actually follow lines that are not directly prior to them in the text. A literary device, or convention, is used to bring together lines that have been separated from each other. The convention is not to be counted an event of the plot. The convention has tagged onto it lines that someone was thinking before they actually appear in the text, and these very same lines also are used to explain an event that occurs later on in the text. This same structure occurs in Hamlet's soliloquy in the prayer scene:

> When he is drunk asleep; or in his rage;
> Or in the incestuous pleasure of his bed;
> At gaming, swearing, or about some act
> That has no relish of salvation in't—

(Act III, scene iii, 92-95)

These lines themselves refer to the reason Hamlet will do something. They do not say what this something is that he will do. We have to look for the line that says what he will do. That line is "I know my course" (Act II, scene ii, 606), meaning that Hamlet will kill Claudius. We see, then, that lines 92-95 in Act III, scene iii, belong right after line 606 in Act II, scene ii, even though the lines are separated in the text by 26 pages. Hamlet is going to kill Claudius (Act II, scene ii, 606) for gambling ("when" means "for"), for swearing (Act III, scene iii, 92-95).

Lines 92-95 are also telling us that Hamlet is going to kill Claudius for something you don't kill someone for: you don't kill someone for gambling. Lines 92-95 also mean that Hamlet plans to kill Claudius without first confronting him and saying, "You killed my father."

Hamlet, because he cannot confront Claudius and take revenge for the reason that Claudius killed his father, is going to kill Claudius without confronting him and for something that you don't kill someone for. These four lines explain why Hamlet is killing someone (Polonius, though Hamlet thought it was Claudius) for eavesdropping. (Lines 76-91 are a convention.)

We are now able to solve the problem we started out with. The play now makes sense. Because Hamlet never ran into Claudius praying, he really did think that it was Claudius behind the arras, and he really was in a mood to kill him.

After writing this paper, I came across two interesting books on the play. One is *Shakespeare's Concept of Tragedy*, by Rocco Montano (Gateway Editions, Chicago, 1985). On page 218, Montano suggests that we consider whether Claudius' prayer is an integral part of the action. He points out that Claudius must have known it was pointless to pray, inasmuch as he was not willing to give up what he got by unlawful means. If it is true that Claudius' prayer is not to be counted one of the events of the plot, then Hamlet's running into Claudius praying is not to be counted one of the events of the plot. The other book is *The Problems of Hamlet* by G.F. Bradby (Oxford University Press, 1928, pp. 31-34). Bradby shows that lines 222-240 of Act III, scene iv, are not to be counted one of the events of the plot. Hamlet, in these lines, is telling his mother that he is being sent to England. Bradby shows that, according to the text, Hamlet could not have known this, and says that these lines were inserted to explain what happens later on in the text, namely, the episode on board ship. This, then, makes three sections in the play that are not part of the plot.

Chapter 10

ഇറ

Sommers' Syllogistic Calculus and Categories

Professor Fred Sommers[1] has made many spectacular discoveries resulting in a calculus that not only handles syllogisms, including relational ones, but also arguments with compound propositions. I would like to make some corrections to his calculus and to his categories.

Professor Sommers says that "all" is a minus, "some" is a plus, "is" is a plus, and "is not" is a minus. He also says that the premises of a valid argument add up to the conclusion. So, for example, the syllogism

> All men are mortal
> Socrates is a man
> _____
> Socrates is mortal

has the form

> -M + P
> -S + M
> _____
> -S + P

The "-M" of the first premise is added to the "+M" of the second premise thereby canceling the two. (Singular terms take either minus or plus.) The correction I would like to make here is that the "-" for "all" is not the minus that is in "-5," but is rather subtraction; that the "+" for "some" is not the plus that is in "+5," but is rather addition; that the "+" for "is" is not plus, but is rather addition; and that the "-" for "is not" is not minus, but is rather subtraction. This means that the premises are not the sort of thing that add up to the conclusion since we do not add an adding or subtracting. Cancellation, then, is an adding and subtracting of the middle term. Therefore, the above syllogism should be written as:

$$-M + P$$
$$-S + M$$
$$\downarrow$$
$$-S + P$$

The following reasons constitute the proof that "All A is B" "subtracts" A and "adds" B:

(1) *The "+" in "+5" is not an operator. The addition sign is an operator. "Is" is an operator. Therefore, "is" is addition, not plus.*
(2) The "+" in "+5" contributes to the value that is "+5." However, "is" does not contribute to the meaning of the predicate term.
(3) If in "All A is B" the "all" were a minus and the "is" a plus, then "All A is B" would not be an assertion. However, it is an assertion. The "all" can be called an act of universalizing and the "is" an act of affirming.
(4) The values "+5" and "-5" are part of a continuum. However, the opposites "is" and "is not" are not.

I would like to make the following points:

(A) There does not seem to be any relation between the subject and the predicate. In "All Socrates is mortal," *"is" does not connect the predicate term to the subject term.* All it does is *operate on the predicate term.*

(B) The statement "No A is B" is regimented as "All (or "each")
    A is not B."

Professor Sommers says that the terms of a syllogism are either positive
or negative and that, therefore, the real logical form of "All A is B," he
says, is -(+A) + (+B). For instance, "green" is really "+green" and
since terms have a negative form (according to Sommers), the negative of
"green" is "non-green" (or "-green"). The following reasons constitute
the proof that terms are neither positive or negative:

(1) "Non-green" does not specify a particular color. Therefore
    it is not a term.
(2) A species cannot be composed of two species of different
    types. Therefore an expression cannot be composed of a
    term and a minus or plus since a term and a plus are two
    things of different types.
(3) You cannot compare two with one. Therefore, you cannot
    compare a minus or a plus and a term and say that they are of
    a different type from an "all" or an "is." Only a term can be
    said to be of a different type from a logical operator. That is,
    "P" and "+" are of different types; "+P" and "+" are not.

I would now like to discuss something that Professor Sommers and
Professor George Englebretsen say about categories. I will use
Englebretsen's book, *Essays on the Philosophy of Fred Sommers*, The
Edwin Mellen Press, 1990, pp. 6-29 as the text. The terms of all syllogisms
comprise the category of physical objects. The terms "men" and "mortal"
in the above syllogism are part of this category. Professor Sommers and
Professor Englebretsen state correctly that if there is at least one term that
makes sense of all entities, then all those entities belong to the same
category. They then claim that there are at least two terms that make
sense of mathematical entities and physical objects. "Interesting" and
"exists," they claim, are two such terms. They conclude that mathematical
entities and physical objects go together to form one grand category. I
believe Sommers and Englebretsen are mistaken. I do not believe that
"interesting" is a term. The term is actually "to be interested in" and
makes sense of human beings and perhaps at least one other species. As
for the term "exists," I do not believe that mathematical entities can be

said to exist, especially if "exists" means "to occupy space." Therefore, there are no terms that make sense of both mathematical entities and physical objects. Therefore, the two do not form one grand category but form two separate categories.

References

1. Sommers, Fred. "The Calculus of Terms," *Mind* 79 (1970): 1-39; "Existence and Predication," *Logic and Ontology*, ed. Milton K. Munitz. New York: New York University Press, 1973, 159-174; "Distribution Matters," *Mind* 84 (1975): 27-46; "Frege or Leibniz?" *Studies on Frege, Vol. III*, ed. Matthias Schirn. Stuttgart Bad Cannstatt: Fromman - Holzboog, 44, 1976; "Logical Syntax in Natural Language," *Issues in the Philosophy of Language*, ed. Alfred F. MacKay and Daniel D. Merrill. New Haven, Connecticut and London: Yale University Press, 1976, 11-41; *The Logic of Natural Language*. Oxford: Clarendon Press, 1982

Chapter 11

৪০০৪

What Was Hamlet's Reason
For Putting on the Play?

There are those who believe that Hamlet put on the play-within-the-play to determine whether Claudius did in fact murder his father, to determine whether the ghost who had told him that Claudius killed his father was deceiving him. I agree with the Freudians, who believe that Hamlet never thought that he had been deceived by the ghost. The three references to the ghost's deceiving him — Act II, scene ii, 606-613; Act III, scene ii, 81-85 and 298-299 (Folger Library Edition) — can only be construed as excuses on Hamlet's part for not having taken revenge against Claudius.

The text bears this out. Hamlet curses himself out in the "O, what a rogue and peasant slave am I!" soliloquy (Act II, scene ii, 555-613). A person would not call himself names if he were not to blame for something. Therefore, Hamlet would not have done this if he really did not know whether the ghost was deceiving him. In this same soliloquy, he says "What would he (the actor who just performed for him) do had he the motive and cue for passion that I have?" (lines 566-568). This shows that Hamlet knows that Claudius killed his father. Further in the soliloquy, he says ". . . for a king, / upon whose property and most dear life / a damned defeat was made" (lines 576-578). Here, too, he is saying his father was murdered. Further in the soliloquy, he says ". . . Bloody, bawdy villain! / Remorseless, treacherous, lecherous, kindless villain!" (lines 587-588). A person who did not know for sure whether Claudius had killed the king would not call him these things. A couple of lines later, Hamlet says ". . . I, the son of a dear father murdered, . . ." (line 591). You cannot be any more explicit than that. Lines 596-597 say ". . . I have heard / That guilty creatures, sitting at a play . . ." Note, Hamlet says *guilty* creatures. This means that he already believes that Claudius is guilty. Then Hamlet says "They have proclaimed their malefactions" (600), then "For murder, though it have no tongue . . ." (601). Note, again, he says "murder." Line 603 has "Play something like the murder of my father." The word "murder" again. We see, then, that the lines I have quoted *contradict* the lines in the same soliloquy "The spirit that I have seen / May be a devil" (606-607) and perhaps "Abuses [deceives] me . . ." (611). A person does not think that his father was murdered and at the same time wonder whether his father was murdered. As I said before, I agree with the Freudians' explanation of this contradiction. (Another explanation is possible. Scholars believe that there may have already been a play *Hamlet*, and that Shakespeare revised it. What the ghost told Hamlet may have been in the original, and Shakespeare may have just left it there for some reason.)

Well, if Hamlet already knew that Claudius had murdered his father, why did he put on the play? The answer is in this same soliloquy. Hamlet says "And can say nothing!" (576). Hamlet was not capable of going over to Claudius and saying to his face, "You murdered my father." By putting on the play, he would not have to do this.

Chapter 12

ഇ)ര

The Structure and Meaning of the To-be-or-not-to-be Speech

I believe I have discovered the solution to the "To be, or not to be" soliloquy. I will leave it to the reader to decide whether my theory is correct.

Let us go right to the soliloquy:

> To be, or not to be, that is the question:
> Whether 'tis nobler in the mind to suffer
> The slings and arrows of outrageous fortune
> or to take arms against a sea of troubles,
> And by opposing end them. To die — to sleep —
> No more; and by a sleep to say we end
> The heartache, and the thousand natural shocks
> That flesh is heir to. 'Tis a consummation
> Devoutly to be wished. To die — to sleep,
> To sleep — perchance to dream: aye, there's the rub!
> For in that sleep of death what dreams may come
> When we have shuffled off this mortal coil,
> Must give us pause. There's the respect
> That makes calamity of so long life.

For who would bear the whips and scorns of time,
The oppressor's wrong, the proud man's contumely,
The pangs of despised love, the law's delay,
The insolence of office, and the spurns
That patient merit of the unworthy takes,
When he himself might his quietus make
With a bare bodkin? Who would these fardels bear,
To grunt and sweat under a weary life,
But that the dread of something after death —
The undiscovered country, from whose bourn
No traveller returns — puzzles the will,
And makes us rather bear those ills we have
Than fly to others that we know not of?
Thus conscience does make cowards of us all,
And thus the native hue of resolution
Is sicklied o'er by the pale cast of thought,
And enterprises of great pith and moment
With this regard their currents turn awry
And lose the name of action.

(Act III, scene i, 64-96)

I see the soliloquy as being composed of five sections. The first section consists of one line - "To be, or not to be, that is the question." The second section consists of four lines beginning with "Whether 'tis nobler in the mind" and ending with "And by opposing end them." The third section begins with "To die — to sleep — / No more" and ends with "That makes calamity of so long life." The fourth section begins with "For who would bear the whips" and ends with "Thus conscience does make cowards of us all." The fifth section begins with "And thus the native hue of resolution" and ends with "And lose the name of action."

The most important section, I believe, is the fifth section. Hamlet says "And thus the native hue of resolution / Is sicklied o'er with the pale cast of thought," the two most important lines of the soliloquy. Hamlet says "resolution." This means that Hamlet has resolved to take revenge against Claudius, the person who has murdered his father. But, then, Hamlet says that this resolution "is sicklied o'er with the pale cast of thought." Now, what does "thought" do? Hamlet had just said: "Thus conscience does make cowards of us all," and before that "the dread of something after death" prevents us from carrying out a resolution to take our own lives. "Conscience" is something separate from the dread referred to. "Thought" plays the role that "conscience" plays. The "thus" in "thus conscience" means "this is how" (not "therefore") and the "thus" in "thus the native hue" means "this is how." The first "thus" refers to "the dread" (of something after death). So "And thus the native hue of resolution / Is sicklied over with the pale cast of thought" says: "This is how the pale cast of thought sicklied over the native hue of resolution." Therefore, we must supply the "how." Since "thus conscience" refers to the dread of something after death, "thus . . . thought" has to refer to the dread of the consequences of taking revenge. (And this dread is giving Hamlet a pale look.)

Some words on structure. The third section has "To die-to sleep" twice, and it appears at the beginning and the half way mark. The fourth section has "Who would bear" twice, and it appears at the beginning and half way mark. The first part of the third section has a conjunction — "heartache, and the thousand natural shocks" and the first part of the fourth section has a conjunction — "whips and scorns." "Dread of something after death" parallels "what dreams may come, / When we have shuffled off this mortal coil." "Puzzles the will" parallels "Must give us pause."

Now I would like to say why, I believe, there are five sections to this soliloquy. The third and fourth sections have the following meaning:

(1) We have misfortunes.
(2) Taking one's life will get rid of them (though taking one's life is not explicit in the third section).
(3) Taking one's life may cause more misfortunes.
(4) This is why we decide not to take our own lives, but rather live with the misfortunes we have.

Now, note these two sections do not say anything about tackling *the misfortunes themselves*. The question in these two sections is whether we should do something *to ourselves*. But the lines that I am calling the second section *do* talk about doing something to the misfortunes themselves. Therefore, the second section has nothing to do with the third and fourth sections. The second section asks whether we should take arms *against a sea of troubles* to end *them*. The action taken would be directed *to the troubles themselves*. There is never any question in this section as to whether we should take our own lives.

The second section also has nothing to do with the first section "To be, or not to be, that is the question," since the first section only asks whether we should exist or not exist, and does not mention doing anything to misfortunes. The first section goes with the third and fourth sections, though more with the third section than with the fourth, it seems.

The second section goes with the fifth section. Both refer to a particular problem itself. The resolution mentioned refers to a particular misfortune or injustice that befell Hamlet and his attempt to do something *to it*. There are other reasons why the second section goes with the fifth section. The second section deals with Hamlet, not with mankind. It has "Whether 'tis nobler in the mind." If it were dealing with mankind, it would not have said "in the mind." I don't think anyone would say "mankind would suffer in the mind." In addition, it says "nobler." Since Hamlet is a prince, he would think of something as being noble or not.

Why are the second and fifth sections in the soliloquy if they have nothing to do with it? I think the answer is that they were *added* to the soliloquy around the year 1603 or 1604. One of those is the year the second version of the play was published. *These two sections do not appear in the first version* we have, which came out in 1602 or 1603.

The first version, called Quarto 1, has the first section, almost verbatim, and a horrendous mixture of the third and fourth sections. Though the quarto has both sections together, there may have been a time when the soliloquy was only composed of the first section and the third section. The first and third sections are not explicit about whether we should take our own lives. They just say "to be, or not to be" and "to die — to sleep." The fourth section is explicit. It says: "When he himself might his quietus make / With a bare bodkin." Note, also, that the first and third sections begin with an infinitive. The reason I said "Thus conscience does make cowards of us all" ends the fourth section rather than begins the fifth section is that the line appears, almost verbatim, in the first quarto.

Note that in this soliloquy Hamlet does not criticize himself, because he will be finally taking his first steps towards revenge - putting on the play.

Chapter 13

ഇന്ദ്ര

The Fields of Aristotelian Metaphysics

In this essay, I discuss the metaphysics of Aristotle's system. I do not discuss the metaphysics of any other system.

In the first field — existence — we list what exists:

> man
> horse
> tree

and millions of other species. Attributes do not go on the list. By extension, the names of the individuals of a species can go on the list. By "exist," we mean "to occupy space." Therefore, telling-the-truth, cities, earthquakes, states of affairs, and numbers cannot be said to exist in this sense. They are not species that occupy space. They exist in the sense that they are derived from species or other physical objects that occupy space.

In the second field — definition — we define words that refer to those species that do exist and define attributes:

> "man" — animal that is rational
> "happy" — enjoying well-being

We cannot define the individuals of a species. "Animal" is called the genus and "rational" the differentia. A separate list lists the physical parts of species, such as biped for man. Another list lists properties, such as capable-of-laughter for man.

In the third field — sense — we put the names of species on one side and the words that signify attributes on the other side, and then we pair each attribute word with two or more species words that it makes sense of:

> man   happy
> horse   heavy
> tree   tall
>   *make sense together*
> man   happy,   heavy,   tall
> horse   happy,   heavy,   tall
> tree   tall,   heavy

The reason that an attribute has to make sense of at least two other species is that each species has to be the same type as at least one other species. By definition, two species A and B are of the same type if whatever makes sense of A makes sense of B and if whatever makes sense of B makes sense of A. If an attribute made sense of only one species, that species would not be the same type as at least one other species. Man is an exception. He has attributes that make sense only of him, e.g., being a genius. Therefore, it seems that a species existed in the distant past that Man was the same type as (or belonged to the same immediate genus as) but died out. (Since Man is currently not the same type as any other species, he does not belong to the same immediate genus that gorillas and chimpanzees belong to — primate.)

Species cannot have attributes of different types. Therefore, if two words that signify attributes of different types make sense of a species, at least one of the two words has to be ambiguous. Two attributes A and B (and two species C and D) are of different types if A makes sense of C but not of D and B makes sense of D but not of C. For example, a tree can be shady but a knife cannot, while a knife can be sharp but a tree cannot. So nothing can be both sharp and shady.

Only species of the same type can combine. There cannot be a man-horse. There can be and is a horse-donkey (mule) since horses and donkeys are of the same type.

Two entities, A and B, are in different categories if nothing that makes sense of A makes sense of B and if nothing that makes sense of B makes sense of A. Therefore, events are in a different category from physical objects. If there is a word that does make sense of entities in two different categories, then it must be ambiguous, e.g., "hard" with respect to chairs and questions. Those categories other than the category of physical objects are derived from the category of physical objects and are therefore not categories in the same sense that the category of physical objects is a category.

Species and attributes form a hierarchy. The hierarchy includes the liquids and gases. The highest genus is "physical object." Is there only one attribute alongside "physical object" that makes sense of every species, or more than one? My guess is that there is more than one — "green," "heavy," and others. I don't think that "exists" is an attribute in the category of physical objects since existence is in the first field and so precedes formation of the hierarchy. Is the ultimate genus "physical object" divided into two subgenera or more than two? My guess is two — animate and inanimate. (Actually, I shouldn't say "in," because "non" is not allowed in Aristotelian metaphysics.)

In the fourth field — syntax — we lay down the rules for forming statements. There are four logical operators: "all" (or "each"), "some," "is," "is not." Species terms (which are picked from a hierarchy, and the hierarchy built up from the definitions) are put after the operators "all" and "some." Attribute terms are put after "is" and "is not." ("No man is perfect" is "Each man is not perfect.") Of course, only those attribute terms and species terms that were able to make it to the make-sense-together list are allowed to form statements. By extension, we allow the names of the individuals of a species to form the subject of a statement. There are terms that are not really subject terms but are allowed to be subject terms in order to make things simple; for example, "ballplayer," "the author of Waverly." If we can say "Some men are ballplayers" and "That man is the author of Waverly," then these two terms are attribute terms. If we didn't allow "ballplayer" to be put after "all" and "some," we would have to say "All men that are ballplayers are . . ." and if we didn't allow "author of Waverly" to be a subject term, we would have to say "Scott, who is the author of Waverly is . . ." Attribute terms such as "happy," "intelligent" are allowed to be subject terms, again, to make things simple. ("Is a physical object," "to be one" are not attribute terms.)

In the sentence "Telling-the-truth is a virtue," let's assume that it is not correct procedure to rephrase it as "All people who tell the truth have a virtue." Then "telling-the-truth" is a "subject." But from the fact that it is a "subject" it does not follow that telling-the-truth exists, since it was determined before we reached the field of syntax that it is only derived from things that exist.

The following is not allowed: "All men are animals." The form "All A are B" is reserved for saying something about all A. When we say "All men are mortal," we are saying what all men are, but when we define "man" as an animal (that is rational), we are not saying what all men are but saying what a man is.

There are two kinds of attribute terms — absolute terms (e.g., "happy") and relational terms (e.g., "loves Mary"). Subject terms and predicate terms can be compound — e.g., "women that are twenty years old," "great ballplayer." Terms are neither positive nor negative. The expression "non-good" is not an attribute since it does not say what something is.

Sentences that are in the passive are not allowed for the reason that they are superfluous. For example, "Mary is loved by John" is really "John loves Mary."

In the fifth field — semantics — we define a statement and we define truth. A statement is an assertion of a state of affairs. We should not define a statement as a sentence that is true or false. First, a definition of a statement should not say what all statements are but what a statement is. "Being true or false" is a property of statements, and properties cannot be part of a definition. Second, a statement cannot be a sentence since a sentence is grammatical or English, whereas a statement is neither. A statement is true if the state of affairs asserted exists.

In the sixth field — logic — we determine whether a syllogism is valid. An example of a syllogism:

> All men are mortal
> Socrates is a man
> Socrates is mortal

The philosopher, Fred Sommers, has discovered a calculus for determining the validity of syllogisms (including those that have relational terms). "All" is subtraction, "some" is addition, "is" is addition and "is not" is subtraction. (Actually, Sommers said "plus" and "minus.") Singular terms ("Socrates," "that man") now have to have an operator — either "all" or "some." The above syllogism is now:

$$-A \quad +B$$
$$-C \quad +A$$
$$\downarrow$$
$$-C \quad +B$$

Sommers' calculus also handles compound statements such as "if p, then q," "p or q," "p and q," but his calculus is not natural for such statements. His calculus is natural for categorical statements (the "all" and "some" statements). (And the propositional-predicate calculus is not natural for syllogistic statements.)

The next field is outside Aristotelian metaphysics. This is the field of everyday discourse. This is the field in which we actually say something about physical objects, the field in which we affirm or deny attributes of physical objects.

Chapter 14

ഇറ

The Semantics of "There Are" Sentences

In this essay I am going to set forth the semantics, or meaning, or function of "there are" sentences.

There is a rule in the English language that requires us to use "there are" sentences when we want to focus just on the thing we are talking about without comparing it, or contrasting it, with other things of that class or group. For example, let us say that there are four cats in a room and that they are all sleeping on a bed, and we don't want to talk about any other cats with respect to that bed. Then we must say

(1)   There are some *cats* sleeping on the bed (Or, some *cats* are sleeping on the bed)

If instead, we say

(2)   **Some* cats are sleeping on the bed

then we are speaking ungrammatically! Sentence (2) is used when we want to compare the thing we are talking about with the other things of that group. In such a situation the rule requires us to use the syllogistic "all," "no," or "some" quantifiers. So, for instance, let us say there are those same four cats, and two of the cats are sleeping on the bed and two are not, and someone asks us how many cats are sleeping on the bed. Then we must say

(3)   *Some* cats are sleeping on the bed

If we want to talk about all four cats, then we would add

(4)   *Some* cats are not sleeping on the bed

If, instead, we had said

(5)   *There are some *cats* sleeping on the bed

we would then have spoken ungrammatically!

Note, that in syllogistic sentences with the verb "to be," the quantifier is stressed while in "there are" sentences the noun is stressed. This makes sense because if you need to compare then you would stress the quantifier and if you do not need to compare you would not stress the quantifier. So in sentence (3) "some" is stressed, while in sentence (1) "cats" is stressed.

Since in syllogistic we are comparing all members of a group to each other, the "all," "no," and "some" are short for "all of the," "none of the," and "some of the." Therefore sentence (3) is really

(6)   Some of the cats are sleeping on the bed

Now in the example of the four cats, if three of the cats are not sleeping on the bed and one is, and we need to do some comparing, then we cannot say

(7)   *Some cats are sleeping on the bed and the others are not

We have to say something like

(8)   One cat is sleeping on the bed and the others are not

Therefore the syllogistic "some" means "two or more of the." (We should really say "each" and "at least one" are syllogistic quantifiers, not "all" and "some.")

Here are some other "there are" sentences:

(9)   There are earthquakes in California
(10) There are no earthquakes in California
(11) There are flaws in your argument
(12) There are no flaws in your argument
(13) There are some suspects being questioned by the police
(14) There are no suspects being questioned by the police

Let us discuss the following sentences:

(15) Several cats are sleeping on the bed
(16) Many cats are sleeping on the bed
(17) Two cats are sleeping on the bed

Are they grammatical? Yes, if you are comparing; no, if your are not. If you do not want to compare you must say :

(18) There are several cats sleeping on the bed
(19) There are many cats sleeping on the bed
(20) There are two cats sleeping on the bed

Now we see why we were all wondering whether sentences such as (15), (16), and (17) are grammatical.

I believe the following sentence is grammatical.

(21) A cat is at the door

Here are two interesting sentences:

(22) There is someone at the door
(23) Someone is at the door

I take it that "someone" in sentence (22) is a compound noun, for if it were a pronoun, the sentence would be ungrammatical. Then why is sentence (23) grammatical? It seems that in sentence (23) "someone" is considered a pronoun, and any sentence whose subject is a pronoun is syllogistic since a pronoun does or can take the place of a proper name, and a sentence whose subject is a proper name is considered syllogistic.[1]

References

1. For a discussion of "there are" sentences, see Milsark, Gary, "Toward an Explanation of Certain Peculiarities of the Existential Construction in English," *Linguistic Analysis* 3 (1977): 1-29

Chapter 15

ഇോയ

The Scientific Method in
Linguistics and Literature

Though each person has a different type of mind, each person uses the scientific method.

I will explain what the scientific method is in linguistics and literature based on the essays in this book on sentences with symmetric verbs and *Hamlet*.

If you have a problem in linguistics, you have to use the scientific method. One problem in the domain (technical term) of sentences with symmetric verbs is where did sentences with the form of (1)

(1)   John and Bill are similar to each other

come from. "To be similar" is symmetric. So why do we have "each other"? It seems redundant. And how did "Bill" get into the subject? Some other sentences in this domain are

(2)   John is similar to Bill
(3)   John and Bill are similar

I was first introduced to this problem about nineteen years ago. I couldn't solve it. About six years later I made another attempt. The reason I wanted to try to solve it again was that I was in a particularly happy mood. At the beginning of the inquiry I had to admit that I did not know how to derive any of the above sentences. I was inclined to believe that (2) was the initial condition (technical term) and that I half felt that (3) came from (1). I thought about this problem every day for two months. My head felt full. I still had not solved the problem. I was about to give up. I then decided to give it one more try. Right after this decision I looked into a book on semantics. The book had something like the following illustration:

(4)   John and Bill box tonight

I could not figure out whether this sentence is symmetric or not. Then I phrased the question "Is it symmetric or is it not?" Because the "is" was close to the "is not" in the question it came to me that the symmetric came from the non-symmetric (actually, semisymmetric). So sentences like (1) came from sentences like (5)

(5)   John and Mary embraced each other

"To embrace" is not symmetric. It is semisymmetric, but in sentence (5) it is used symmetrically. The verb by itself is semisymmetric because a person can start to embrace before someone else, but in sentence (5) neither John nor Mary started first. The process through which sentence (1) came from sentence (5) is called analogy. When we claim that sentence (1) came from sentence (5), we are said to offer an hypothesis (technical term). An hypothesis is an explanation of an event by giving its cause. The set of hypotheses in a domain is called a theory (technical term). Sentence (1) was the central sentence or event. It was now easy to determine which sentences came before it and which after it. Sentence (3) came from sentence (1) and sentence (6)

(6)   John and Mary embraced

came from sentence (3) — by analogy. Sentence (5) came from sentence (7)

(7)   John embraced Mary and Mary embraced John

An added attraction to a theory in science is the discovery of a novel (technical term) phenomenon. Sentence (7) is novel since we did not know that such a sentence ever existed and that it had a symmetric meaning.

In linguistics it is very important to know whether a sentence is an exception (technical term) or a counterexample (technical term). In the physical sciences it is called an anomaly (technical term). One exception in the domain of symmetric verb sentences is:

(8)   *John and Mary resemble

This is not a grammatical sentence even though we can say

(9)   John and Mary resemble each other

The explanation is that we adopted a rule from French even though it conflicted with a rule in English. "To resemble" in French is "se ressembler." We borrowed the verb from French in the twelfth century. "Se" means "each other." There is a rule in French that if "se" is part of a verb, it cannot be deleted. We borrowed this rule. So we see that sentence (8) is not a counterexample. I would like to add that I believe that a person can be said to know a domain or topic even though he does not know the explanation of an exception.

Domains have auxiliary hypotheses (technical term). One example of an auxiliary hypothesis is that whenever a sentence comes from another sentence it is synonymous with that sentence (analogy is an exception). Sentences (1) and (3) confirm (technical term) this. This auxiliary hypothesis can also be used to prove that a certain hypothesis cannot be right. For instance, the hypothesis that

(10) John agreed with Bill

came from

(11) John and Bill agreed

cannot be correct since these two sentences are not synonymous ((10) is not symmetric, (11) is). The reasoning is thus:

If a sentence comes from another sentence, then it is synonymous with that other sentence. Sentence (10) is not synonymous with sentence (11). Therefore sentence (10) did not come from sentence (11).

The first premise is the auxiliary hypothesis and is arrived at through induction (technical term). Here induction is generalization based upon one or more cases of observation (technical term). I believe that not all cases have to be observed. The second premise is gotten by observation. The conclusion is gotten by deduction (technical term). Obviously, we first have to have induction in order to have deduction. In the physical sciences deduction is also used to deduce the consequences (technical term). We then conduct an experiment (technical term) to see if the consequences come out true.

Domains have background knowledge (technical term). In the domain of symmetric verb sentences it consists of facts like "to be similar" is a symmetric verb, "to embrace" is semisymmetric, "John and Mary are similar" is synonymous with "John and Mary are similar to each other," "John and Mary left" is not synonymous with "John and Mary left with each other," and "John is similar to Mary" is grammatical. Obviously, we have to have our facts right in order to solve a problem. I would like to add that I don't think we have to know all the facts in order to solve a problem. I was not sure, and still am not sure, whether "to collide" and "to meet" are symmetric, but this did not prevent me from solving the problem.

The prerequisites of a good hypothesis are:

(A)   It should be simple. The least number of steps in a derivation is preferred. An hypothesis involving just one step is preferable to one involving sixteen steps. ("Simplicity" is a technical term.)

(B)   It often involves familiar causes. Analogy and deletion are two such causes.

(C)   In the physical sciences one hypothesis (or theory) is better than another hypothesis if it explains more phenomena than the other hypothesis.

(D)   It should have the form of an explanation rather than the form of a description. For example, in trying to explain how sentences such as "John and Bill are similar to each other" came into being, we should not say, "Well, English has sentences in which the subject consists of two proper names joined by the conjunction *and*."

(E) It often does not conflict with the background knowledge, auxiliary hypotheses, and initial conditions.

I would now like to discuss my use of the scientific method in reading Shakespeare's *Hamlet*. (See Chapter 9 of this book, "Is the Prayer Scene in *Hamlet* Part of the Plot?")

About twenty two years ago, a lady friend introduced me to the play. I read it but without any intention of mastering it. Something about the play must have bothered me, for ten years later I read it again. But this time I read the play with intensity in order to master it. And while I read the play, I myself was in a Hamlet-like situation, though I was not conscious of this. There were people in my life at this time who were like Claudius, Gertrude, Polonius, Horatio, and Ophelia. I was like Hamlet. The person who was like Claudius mistreated me but I did not respond. A short time after this I read the following four lines in the play:

When he is drunk asleep; or in his rage;
Or in the incestuous pleasure of his bed;
At gaming, swearing, or about some act
That has no relish of salvation in't-
(Act III, scene iii, 92-95, Folger Library edition)

I did not read these lines with any special understanding. After a short time passed, the person who was like Claudius said something to me that had nothing wrong with it. I responded by talking back to him, as though there were something wrong. That night I went to sleep. The following morning, a few hours after I had gotten up, a smile formed on my lips, and I blurted out to the person who was like Horatio what the above quoted lines mean. What Hamlet is saying in those four lines is that since he cannot take revenge against Claudius for the specific reason that Claudius did something wrong to him — namely, murdered his father — he is going to kill Claudius when Claudius is not doing anything wrong to him or is doing something you don't kill someone for. (If Claudius were to swear, he would not be doing anything wrong to Hamlet.) My subconscious mind remembered how I responded the previous day and saw that what happened in those four lines was the same thing that happened to me the day before. The seeing of a similarity is observation.

Chapter 16

ഇരുൽ

More on "There Are" Sentences

There are two basic types of "there are" sentences-locatives and non-locatives. Locatives are divided into two subtypes and non-locatives are divided into at least four subtypes.

| Locatives: | (1) | physical object |
| | (2) | non-physical object |

Non-Locatives:	(3)	preposition
	(4)	clause
	(5)	verbal noun
	(6)	past participle

Here are some examples:
(1) There is a cat on the bed
     There are some cats sleeping on the bed
(2) There is an earthquake in California
     There is a flaw in your argument
(3) There is evidence for your theory
     There is an argument between John and Mary

(4)   There is no evidence that he did it
       There is no doubt that he did it
(5)   There is no holding Tiger Woods
       There is much wringing of the hands
(6)   There are some students loved by Mary
       There are more than 3,700 religions practiced by Americans

Basic "there are" sentences are non-syllogistic. They are opposed to syllogistic sentences in function, or meaning. Basic "there are" sentences do not compare the individuals of a group with other individuals of that group, whereas syllogistic sentences do with their "all," "some," and proper name-subjects. Another "there are" sentence but without the words "there are" is "Some *cats* are sleeping on the bed," and another is "Some *cats* are on the bed."

Here is a list of non-basic "there are" sentences:

(7)   There are *some* theologians who . . .
(8)   There followed the name of the university
(9)   There were the sharks circling the cage

Non-basic "there are" sentences are syllogistic. I am saying (7) is syllogistic because we are stressing "some," which we do in a syllogistic sentence beginning with "some." I am saying (8) is syllogistic because "the name of the university" seems to be acting like a proper name-subject. Sentence (9) was uttered by a woman who was listing the difficulties she had in swimming from Cuba to Florida. It seems to me syllogistic for the same sort of reason that (8) is syllogistic.

There is another "there are" sentence which I will classify as one created by certain philosophers. A syllogistic sentence such as "*Some* cats are on the bed" is regimented as "There is at least one thing that is a cat and is on the bed."

It seems to me that we now have an actual starting point from which to attempt to determine the origin of "there are" sentences. Did they come from sentences such as "A God is," or "Some *cats* are on the bed," or "A cat is on the bed," or "On the bed is a cat"?

This essay was written in 1997. In January 1998 I read a discussion by George Lakoff[1] on the syntax of "there are" sentences. His theory is that a sentence such as

(10) There is a cat sleeping on the bed

actually came from two clauses or sentences

(11) There is a cat. A cat is sleeping on the bed.

or

(12) There is a cat that is sleeping on the bed.

So "sleeping on the bed" in (10) is really a separate clause or sentence with "that" being deleted. The "is" in (10) does not go with "sleeping." In (12), the first sentence introduces the cat, and the second sentence refers back to it. This enables Lakoff to handle a sentence such as

(13) There is a fire in the basement

It came from

(14) There is a fire which is in the basement.

His theory has an advantage over other theories. Another theory might derive (10) from

(15) A cat is sleeping on the bed

but it wouldn't be able to derive (13) because

(16) *A fire is in the basement

is ungrammatical. I like Lakoff's theory. I just have one doubt at this point. Is a sentence such as

(17) There is a cat that is sleeping on the bed

grammatical or not? And if it is grammatical, wouldn't it be ungrammatical to delete "that is"?

In March of 1998 a theory came to me. Permit me to express it. Sentences such as (18)

(18) *An earthquake is in California

is ungrammatical because events cannot be in a place or be in a place the way physical objects can be. I would say that to avoid uttering a sentence such as (18) we used a verb to show the relationship between the event and the place. So we uttered a sentence like (19)

(19) An earthquake is occurring in California

As for a sentence like (20),

(20) There is an earthquake in California

perhaps it came from sentences such as (21)

(21) There is a cat on the bed

by analogy. (The meaning of "occur" is implied in (20), and (19) is sometimes syllogistic and sometimes existential.) Of course, we would still need a theory for the origin of sentences such as (21) and for the non-locative existential sentences.

References

1. Lakoff, George. *Women, Fire, and Dangerous Things: What Categories Reveal about the Mind*. Chicago, Illinois: University of Chicago Press, 1987

Chapter 17

ഇ◯ര

When Did Hamlet Think of Putting on the Play?

The theme of Act I is the finding out by Hamlet, Prince of Denmark, that his father, the king, has been murdered and the finding out by Hamlet that Claudius, his uncle, was the murderer. The theme of Act II is Hamlet's taking his first steps towards taking revenge against Claudius. Two months had passed before Hamlet started to take revenge. We know this because Ophelia, his girl friend, says that Hamlet's father died "twice two months (ago)," Act III, Scene II, 136 (in The New Folger Library Edition), and Hamlet says "two months dead, nay, not so much, not two," Act I, Scene II, 142, which means he found out about the murder two months after it occurred. During the two months after he found out about the murder, he was weak and melancholy (Act II, Scene II, 630). Also, Polonius, the counselor to Claudius, tells us that Hamlet was (during these two months) in a sadness, then a fast, then a watch, then a weakness, then a lightness, and then into a madness in which he raved (Act II, Scene II, 156-159).

Hamlet decides to put on a play at night in which he will indirectly accuse the king of murdering his father and then will kill him that same night. I like to think he had this plan before Rosencrantz and Guildenstern, his friends, visited him. (Commentators think it was during the visit.)

My reasons are:

(1) Hamlet tells Rosencrantz and Guildenstern that Man does not delight him. Rosencrantz replies ". . . if you delight not in man, what lenten entertainment (miserable reception) the players (actors) shall receive from you. We coted (passed) them on the way, and hither are they coming to offer you service," Act II, Scene II, 339-342. Note, Rosencrantz says "*the* players." "The" means that Hamlet already knew that the actors were coming. Since he already knew the actors were coming, he thought of the idea of putting on the play before his friends visited him. There is something that bothers me, though. Rosencrantz tells Hamlet's mother, the queen, (Gertrude) that ". . . it so fell out that certain players / We o'erraught (overtook) on the way. Of these we told him . . ." (Act III, Scene I, 17-18). Here it sounds as though Hamlet did not know about the players' coming. Perhaps, though, Rosencrantz was speaking loosely.

(2) When the actors arrive, Polonius says to Hamlet "The actors are come hither," Act II, Scene II, 416. Note, he also says "the." Note, Polonius was not with Hamlet and his friends during their meeting, so he would not have known that the players' coming was discussed. Again, he would not have said "the" if he thought Hamlet did not know the players were coming.

(3) As soon as Rosencrantz mentions that the players are coming, Hamlet immediately says "He that plays the king shall be welcome. . . ," Act II, Scene II, 343. It seems that Hamlet already knows the make-up of the troupe.

(4) Hamlet asks an actor if he could study a speech of some dozen or sixteen lines that he would set down and insert into the play (Act II, Scene II, 566-568). How could Hamlet have known how many lines he would write? It seems that he had already written one version of some twelve lines and one of some sixteen lines.

(5) Hamlet put on an antic disposition (played a fool) in order to ensure his plan would work. Therefore, he had the plan before he put on the antic disposition. And since he put on the antic disposition before his friends visited him, he thought of the plan of putting on the play and of taking revenge before his friends visited him. That is, Hamlet thought of putting on the play "between Act I and Act II."

Chapter 18

ഇറ

The Origin of Existential Sentences

I have discovered the origin of existential sentences! And I am very happy. It was not easy. It took two or three years of study.

There are two varieties of existential sentences: the "there" variety and the "some" variety. The "some" variety came first:

(1)   A cat is on the bed
(2)   Some cats are on the bed

In (2), "some" is unstressed and "cats" stressed. Now, at this time in the English language, we had a rule that allowed us to reverse the order of the subject and the material after the verb. For example, instead of

(3)   The Lord spoke thus

we could say

(4)   Thus spoke the Lord

So, instead of

(5)   A cat is on the bed

we could say

(6)   On the bed is a cat

Sentences (5) and (6) are existential. We are not comparing one cat with the other cats of the world as we do in a syllogistic sentence. Examples of syllogistic sentences are:

(7)   All cats are intelligent
(8)   No cats are intelligent
(9)   Some cats are intelligent
(10) Some cats are not intelligent

In sentences (7) to (10), the cats of the world are being compared. In (9), "some" is stressed and "cats" unstressed.

But, now, let's say we wanted to contradict the aforementioned existential sentences. I think that at that time we did not use the word "no" for existential sentences. What we may have used is "not a." So, the contradictory, then, of

(11) A cat is on the bed

was, perhaps,

(12) Not a cat is on the bed

But, now, we wanted to form the contradictory of

(13) On the bed is a cat

But how did we form it? It looks as though the Reversal Rule did not allow us to reverse the subject and the post verbal material when the subject had "not a." So that even though we could say

(14) Not a cat is on the bed

we could not say

(15) *On the bed is not a cat

Therefore, some way had to be invented to enable us to form the contradictory for

(16) On the bed is a cat

It looks as though we took sentence (16) and added "there" to the left of "on the bed" and added "not" between "is" and "a." Hence, sentence (17):

(17) There on the bed is not a cat

So, sentence (17) was the first "there" existential sentence! Note that "there on the bed" is a kind of subject, "is" is a verb, and "not a cat" is a kind of post verbal material. And "there" has the meaning of place! But, now, we were allowed to apply the Reversal Rule to sentence (17) coming up with

(18) Not a cat is there on the bed

Sentence (18) proves that there was once such a sentence as sentence (17).

We did not say

(19) *There on the bed is a cat

There was no reason to. Sentence (16) was sufficient. And since we never created sentence (19), it is ungrammatical. So is

(20) *A cat is there on the bed

since there was no sentence for it to be a reverse of. After sentence (21)

(21) There on the bed is not a cat

was in existence for a while, and, perhaps, because, by then, "there" lost its meaning of place in this sentence, we moved "on the bed" to the end of the sentence forming

(22) There is not a cat on the bed

Sentence (22) replaced sentence (21) in the act of moving "on the bed."
Sentence (21) did not remain. It became ungrammatical. The "there" and
"on the bed" had nothing to do with each other anymore. Then, from
sentence (22) we got

(23) There is a cat on the bed

by analogy! It was, perhaps, at this point that we started to use the word
"no" and, so, sentence (22) became

(24) There is no cat on the bed

Sentence (24) replaced sentence (22) for the most part. Note, the Reversal
Rule applies to sentence (21) but not to sentences (22), (23), and (24).
And note that sentence (23) came into existence some time *after* sentences
(21) and (22)!
    The derivation of

(25) There are some cats on the bed

is perhaps:

    a.   Some cats are on the bed
    b   On the bed are some cats
    c.   There on the bed is not a cat
    d.   There is not a cat on the bed
    e.   There are some cats on the bed

Sentence (25)e. was, perhaps, formed from sentence (25)d. by analogy.
Then, from sentence (25)d., we got

    f.   There are no cats on the bed

Sentence (25)f. replaced sentence (25)d. for the most part. Sentence
(25)c. no longer exists. The derivation of

(26) There is a cat sleeping on the bed

is:

a.   A cat is sleeping on the bed
b.   Sleeping on the bed is a cat
c.   There sleeping on the bed is not a cat
d.   There is not a cat sleeping on the bed
e.   There is a cat sleeping on the bed

Sentence (26)e. came from sentence (26)d. by analogy. Then, from sentence (26)d. we got

f.   There is no cat sleeping on the bed

Sentence (26)f. replaced sentence (26)d. for the most part. Sentence (26)c. no longer exists. When sentences (24), (25)f., and (26)f. were formed, the contradictory of sentence (11) became

(27) No cat is on the bed

replacing sentence (12) for the most part. And, if the contradictory of sentence (2) was

(28) Not a cat is on the bed

then this contradictory was changed to

(29) No cats are on the bed

The derivation of

(30) There were some students questioned

is perhaps:

a.   The police questioned some students in the courtyard
b.   In the courtyard, the police questioned some students
c.   Some students were questioned by the police in the courtyard
d.   Questioned by the police in the courtyard were some students
e.   There questioned by the police in the courtyard was not a student

    f.   There was not a student questioned by the police in the courtyard

    g.   There were some students questioned by the police in the courtyard

    h.   There were some students questioned by the police

    i.   There were some students questioned

Sentence (30)g. was formed by analogy from sentence (30)f. Sentence (30)e. no longer exists. (Sentences (30)a. and (30)b. are syllogistic, though the direct object in them is existential.)

Existential sentences that begin with "there flew," "there remains," and so on, may have a derivation similar to the above ones.

Other kinds of existential sentences may have come into existence by analogy from a sentence with the form of (23). Such sentences are:

(31) There is no doubt that he did it

(32) There is evidence that he did it

(33) There is a mistake in your argument

(34) There is an earthquake in California

(35) There is no going back

A popular theory called the "there"-insertion rule suggests, or states, that

(36) There is a cat on the bed

came directly from

(37) A cat is on the bed

by movement of the subject and insertion of "there," and that

(38) There is no cat on the bed

came directly from

(39) No cat is on the bed

But this theory cannot explain why

    (40) Not a cat is there on the bed

is grammatical.

Bibliography

America, a magazine, October 6, 1973

Aristotle. *Categories*

_____. *Metaphysics*

_____. *Topics*

Baedeker, Kurt. *Baedeker's Egypt 1929.* New York: Hippocrene Books, 1985; London: David & Charles Ltd., 1985

Baines, John & Jaromir Malek. *Atlas of Ancient Egypt.* New York: Facts on File, 1980

Bradby, Geoffrey Fox. *The Problems of Hamlet.* New York: Haskell House, 1965; Oxford: Oxford University Press, 1928

Breasted, James Henry. *History of Egypt.* New York: Scribner, 1909

_____. *Decennial Publications of Chicago University,* Series 1, vol. V, 1927

Dougherty, Ray C. "A Survey of Linguistic Methods and Arguments," *Foundations of Language* 10 (1973): 423-490

Elliott, Ralph Warren Victor. *Runes.* New York: Philosophical Library, 1959

Englebretsen, George. *Essays on the Philosophy of Fred Sommers.* Lewiston, New York: The Edwin Mellen Press, 1990

Gleitman, Lila. "Coordinating Conjunctions in English," *Language* 41 (1965): 260-293

Joyce, Donovan. *The Jesus Scroll.* New York: Dial Press, 1973; New York: New American Library, 1974; London: Sphere Books, 1975

Lakoff, George and Stanley Peters. "Phrasal Conjunction and Symmetric Predicates," *Modern Studies in English,* ed. David A. Reibel and Sanford A. Schane. Englewood Cliffs, New Jersey: Prentice Hall, 1969, 113-142

Lakoff, George. *Women, Fire, and Dangerous Things: What Categories Reveal about the Mind.* Chicago, Illinois: University of Chicago Press, 1987

Lehmann, Anne. "Two Sets of Perfect Syllogisms," *Notre Dame Journal of Formal Logic* 14 (1973): 425-429

Lichtheim, Miriam. *Ancient Egyptian Literature, Vol. II, The New Kingdom.* Berkeley and Los Angeles, California; London: University of California Press, 1976

Massey, Gerald. "Tom, Dick and Harry and All the King's Men," *American Philosophical Quarterly* 13 (1976): 89-107

Milsark, Gary. "Toward an Explanation of Certain Peculiarities of the Existential Construction," *Linguistic Analysis* 3 (1977): 1-29

Montano, Rocco. *Shakespeare's Concept of Tragedy.* Chicago, Illinois: Gateway Editions, 1985

Publishers Weekly, a magazine, October 1, 1973

Quine, Willard Van Orman. "Two Dogmas of Empiricism," *From A Logical Point of View.* Cambridge, Massachusetts: Harvard University Press, 1953, 1961, 1980, 20-46

_____. *Word and Object*. Cambridge, Massachusetts: MIT Press, 1960

Shakespeare, William. *Hamlet*. Folger Library Edition

Sommers, Fred. "The Ordinary Language Tree," *Mind* 68 (1959): 160-185

_____. "Types and Ontology," *Philosophical Review* 72 (1963): 327-363

_____. "Predicability," *Philosophy in America*, ed. Max Black. Ithaca, New York: Cornell University Press, 1965, 262-281

_____. "The Calculus of Terms," *Mind* 79 (1970): 1-39

_____. "Structural Ontology," *Philosophia* 1 (1971): 21-42

_____. "Existence and Predication," *Logic and Ontology*, ed. Milton K. Munitz. New York: New York University Press, 1973, 159-174

_____. "Distribution Matters," *Mind* 84 (1975): 27-46

_____. "Frege or Leibniz?" *Studies on Frege, Vol. III*, ed. Matthias Schirn. Stuttgart Bad Cannstatt: Fromman-Holzboog, 44, 1976

_____. "Logical Syntax in Natural Language," *Issues in the Philosophy of Language*, ed. Alfred F. MacKay and Daniel E. Merrill. New Haven, Connecticut and London: Yale University Press, 1976, 11-41

_____. *The Logic of Natural Language*. Oxford: Clarendon Press, 1982

Time, a magazine, December 24, 1972

Wagenknecht, Edward. *The Personality of Shakespeare*. Norman, Oklahoma: University of Oklahoma Press, 1972

Waismann, Friedrich. *The Principles of Linguistic Philosophy*, ed. R. Harre. New York: St. Martin's Press, 1965; London: Macmillan, 1965

Index